Seashore

of the •

Pacific
Northwest

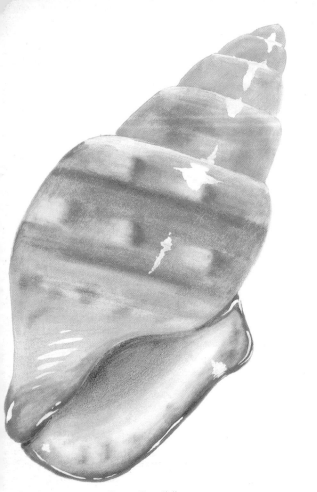

Carinate Dove Shell

Seashore

of the •
Pacific
Northwest

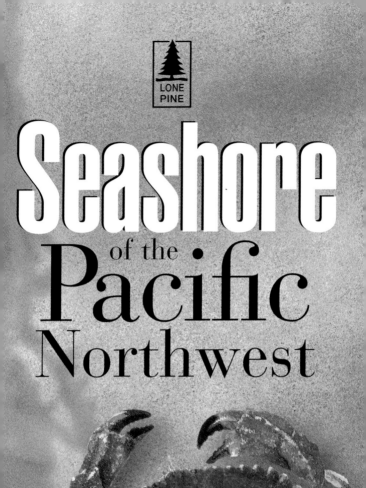

Ian Sheldon

The Publisher: Lone Pine Publishing

1808–B Street NW, Suite 140
Auburn, WA 98001
USA

10145–81 Avenue
Edmonton, AB T6E 1W9
Canada

Lone Pine Publishing website:
http://www.lonepinepublishing.com

Canadian Cataloguing in Publication Data

Sheldon, Ian
     Seashore of the Pacific Northwest

     ISBN-10: 1-55105-161-3
     ISBN-13: 978-1-55105-161-1

     1. Seashore biology—Northwest, Pacific. I. Title.
QH95.7.S535 1998   591.7699'09745   C98-910762-0

Senior Editor: Nancy Foulds
Editors: Nancy Foulds, Rachel Fitz, Lee Craig
Production Manager: David Dodge
Design: Rob Weidemann
Layout and Production: Rob Weidemann
Cover Illustration: Ian Sheldon
Cartography: Rob Weidemann
Illustrations: Ian Sheldon
Separations and Film: Elite Lithographers, Edmonton, Alberta, Canada

The publisher gratefully acknowledges the assistance of the Department of Canadian Heritage.

PC: P3

To the oceans,
for giving birth to beautiful life

To my parents,
for letting me roam untethered

To Jim Butler,
for his guiding spirit

CONTENTS

Bat Star

CONTENTS

MAMMALS

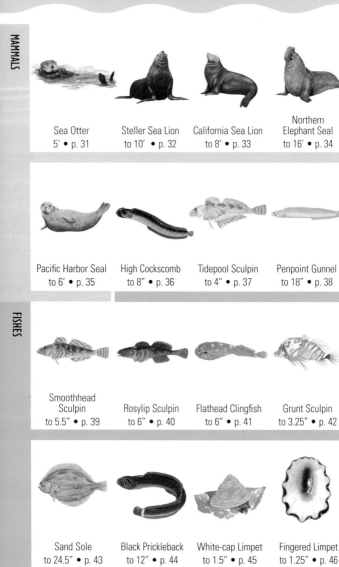

Sea Otter
5' • p. 31

Steller Sea Lion
to 10' • p. 32

California Sea Lion
to 8' • p. 33

Northern
Elephant Seal
to 16' • p. 34

Pacific Harbor Seal
to 6' • p. 35

High Cockscomb
to 8" • p. 36

Tidepool Sculpin
to 4" • p. 37

Penpoint Gunnel
to 18" • p. 38

FISHES

Smoothhead
Sculpin
to 5.5" • p. 39

Rosylip Sculpin
to 6" • p. 40

Flathead Clingfish
to 6" • p. 41

Grunt Sculpin
to 3.25" • p. 42

Sand Sole
to 24.5" • p. 43

Black Prickleback
to 12" • p. 44

White-cap Limpet
to 1.5" • p. 45

Fingered Limpet
to 1.25" • p. 46

LIMPETS

File Limpet
to 1.75" • p. 47

Rough
Keyhole Limpet
to 2.75" • p. 48

Mask Limpet
to 2" • p. 49

Pacific
Plate Limpet
to 2.5" • p. 50

Japanese Abalone
to 7" • p. 51

Frilled Dogwinkle
to 4" • p. 52

Emarginate
Dogwinkle
to 1" • p. 53

Channeled
Dogwinkle
to 1.5" • p. 54

Dire Whelk
to 2" • p. 55

Sculptured
Rocksnail
to 0.75" • p. 56

Lurid Rocksnail
to 1.5" • p. 57

Carinate Dove
Shell
0.4" • p. 58

Oregon Triton
to 6" • p. 59

Leafy Thorn
Purpura
to 3.5" • p. 60

Mudflat Snail
to 1.5" • p. 61

Giant Pacific
Bittium
0.75" • p. 62

Tinted Wentletrap
0.6" • p. 63

Ringed Topshell
to 1.25" • p. 64

Western Ribbed
Topshell
to 1" • p. 65

Red Turban
to 2.25" • p. 66

Dusky Tegula
to 1.5" • p. 67

Black Tegula
to 1.75" • p. 68

Dall's Dwarf Turban
0.4" • p. 69

Tucked Lirularia
to 0.25" • p. 70

SNAILS

Checkered
Periwinkle
to 0.5" • p. 71

Sika Periwinkle
to 0.8" • p. 72

Purple Dwarf Olive
to 1.25" • p. 73

Lewis's Moonsnail
to 5.5" • p. 74

BIVALVES

Pacific Pink Scallop
3.25" • p. 75

Giant Rock Scallop
to 10" • p. 76

Pacific Shipworm
shell 0.25" •
p. 77

Baltic Macoma
to 1.5" • p. 78

Bent-nosed
Macoma
to 3" • p. 79

White Sand
Macoma
to 4.5" • p. 80

Geoduck
to 8" • p. 81

Smooth
Washington Clam
to 5.25" • p. 82

Fat Gaper
to 8" • p. 83

Nuttall's Cockle
to 5.5" • p. 84

Common Pacific
Littleneck
to 3" • p. 85

Japanese
Littleneck
to 3" • p. 86

Pacific Razor Clam
7" • p. 87

Native
Pacific Oyster
to 3.5" • p. 88

Giant
Pacific Oyster
to 12" • p. 89

California Mussel
to 8" • p. 90

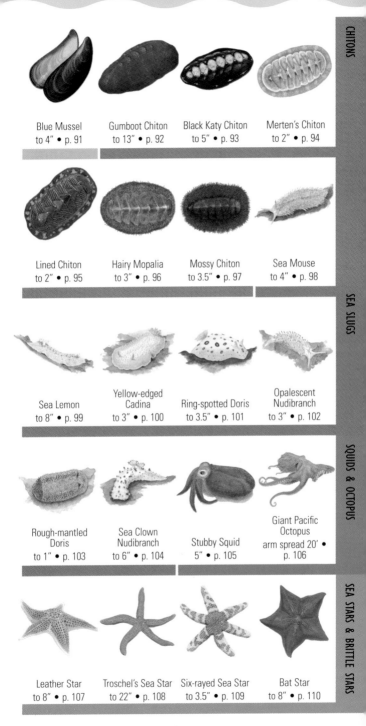

CHITONS

Blue Mussel
to 4" • p. 91

Gumboot Chiton
to 13" • p. 92

Black Katy Chiton
to 5" • p. 93

Merten's Chiton
to 2" • p. 94

Lined Chiton
to 2" • p. 95

Hairy Mopalia
to 3" • p. 96

Mossy Chiton
to 3.5" • p. 97

Sea Mouse
to 4" • p. 98

SEA SLUGS

Sea Lemon
to 8" • p. 99

Yellow-edged
Cadina
to 3" • p. 100

Ring-spotted Doris
to 3.5" • p. 101

Opalescent
Nudibranch
to 3" • p. 102

SQUIDS & OCTOPUS

Rough-mantled
Doris
to 1" • p. 103

Sea Clown
Nudibranch
to 6" • p. 104

Stubby Squid
5" • p. 105

Giant Pacific
Octopus
arm spread 20' •
p. 106

SEA STARS & BRITTLE STARS

Leather Star
to 8" • p. 107

Troschel's Sea Star
to 22" • p. 108

Six-rayed Sea Star
to 3.5" • p. 109

Bat Star
to 8" • p. 110

11

REFERENCE GUIDE

SEA STARS & BRITTLE STARS

Ochre Sea Star
to 14" • p. 111

Sunflower Star
to 40" • p. 112

Daisy Brittle Star
to 3" • p. 113

Eccentric
Sand Dollar
to 3.2" • p. 114

SEA URCHINS

Green Sea Urchin
to 4" • p. 115

Red Sea Urchin
to 5" • p. 116

Purple Sea Urchin
to 3.5" • p. 117

Red Sea Cucumber
10" • p. 118

SEA CUCUMBERS

JELLYFISH

California
Stichopus
to 16" • p. 119

Moon Jelly
to 15" • p. 120

Aggregating
Anemone
3.5" • p. 121

Giant Green
Anemone
to 10" • p. 122

ANEMONES & CORAL

Proliferating
Anemone
to 2" • p. 123

Frilled Anemone
to 18" • p. 124

Painted Urticina
to 5" • p. 125

Orange Cup Coral
to 0.4" • p. 126

CRABS

Red Crab
to 4.25" • p. 127

Dungeness Crab
to 6.4" • p. 128

Purple Shore Crab
to 2" • p. 129

Black-clawed
Mud Crab
1" • p. 130

Flat Porcelain Crab
to 1" • p. 131

Shield-backed
Kelp Crab
to 4.75" • p. 132

Blue-handed
Hermit Crab
to 0.75" • p. 133

Hairy Hermit Crab
to 0.75" • p. 134

Acorn Barnacle
0.6" • p. 135

Giant
Acorn Barnacle
to 4" • p. 136

Thatched Barnacle
to 2" • p. 137

Common
Goose Barnacle
to 6" • p. 138

Leaf Barnacle
to 3.25" • p. 139

Srnooth
Skeleton Shrimp
to 2" • p. 140

Vosnesensky's
Isopod
to 1.4" • p. 141

California Beach
Flea
to 1.1" • p. 142

Coon-stripe Shrimp
to 6" • p. 143

Lug Worm
to 6" • p. 144

Fifteen-scaled
Worm
to 2.5" • p. 145

Red Tube Worm
to 4" • p. 146

Curly
Terebellid Worm
to 11" • p. 147

Six-lined
Nemertean
to 3.3' • p. 148

Stearn's
Sea Spider
5.1" • p. 149

Kelp Encrusting
Bryozoan
variable • p. 150

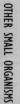

OTHER SMALL ORGANISMS

Staghorn Bryozoan
to 4" • p. 151

Boring Sponge
to 12" • p. 152

Purple Sponge
to 36" • p. 153

Velvety Red
Sponge
to 36" • p. 154

Sea Pork
to 8" • p. 155

Monterey Stalked
Tunicate
to 10" • p. 156

Wrinkled
Sea Squirt
to 2" • p. 157

Winged Kelp
to 10' • p. 158

ALGAE & SEAWEED

Sugar Wrack
to 6' • p. 159

Feather Boa
to 15' • p. 160

Giant
Perennial Kelp
to 40' • p. 161

Bull Kelp
to 80' • p. 162

Sea Palm
to 20" • p. 163

Black Pine
to 12" • p. 164

Little Rockweed
to 6" • p. 165

Rockweed
to 20" • p. 166

Fir Needle
to 10" • p. 167

Tar Spot
to 8" • p. 168

Sea Staghorn
to 16" • p. 169

Enteromorpha
Green Algae
to 10" • p. 170

REFERENCE GUIDE

ALGAE & SEAWEED

Sea Lettuce
to 20" • p. 171

Nail Brush
to 3" • p. 172

Turkish Towel
to 18" • p. 173

Sea Sac
to 6" • p. 174

Iridescent
Seaweed
to 36" • p. 175

Coralline Algae
to 4" • p. 176

Encrusting Coral
variable • p. 177

Surf Grass
to 36" • p. 178

OTHER

Eelgrass
to 36" • p. 179

Blobs of Tar
variable • p. 180

Introduction

The temptations are always there—a beautiful coast, some rocks, some tidepools. For most of us, a walk along the beach or a holiday on the coast brings many joys. As a child, who could resist picking up that strange stringy seaweed cast ashore by the waves, or peering into a rocky tidepool and giggling at the shy hermit crabs? For some of us, the curiosity lives with us always.

The shoreline is incredibly diverse, from extensive sandy beaches to vertical cliffs, from craggy rocks to quiet bays. In all these different landscapes wildlife abounds. The wonderful thing about it all is that it gives us a chance to glimpse into the ocean, a world with which we are not familiar, terrestrial animals that we are. As the tide recedes, creatures are exposed and many of them bear no resemblance to those on land. Is it a plant or animal? Maybe it is just a piece of rock. Maybe something lives in it. There are many beautiful mysteries waiting to be uncovered, waiting to be solved.

As you walk towards the shore, smell the sweetness of the sea, feel the salty spray against your skin and sway to the soothing motion of the waves washing back and forth, remember that you are on the edge of another world. Let yourself go and discover some of the secrets of our coasts and the creatures within. The rewards are tremendous.

California Beach Flea

About This Book

No trip to the coast or wind-swept walk along a beach is complete without a nature guide to tell you just what it is you are looking at. Secrets abound, and while you may know that you are holding a sand dollar, do you really know what a sand dollar is and what it does with its life? This book is an easy guide to help you discover some of the stories behind the strange objects and animals found along the coasts of British Columbia and the Pacific Northwest.

Included in the guide are some of the plants and animals you are likely to encounter as you gaze into a tide-pool or wade through an Eelgrass meadow. This guide is by no means exhaustive. If you had all the guides to everything you might encounter, you would probably need a truck to bring them all in. This book covers the basics: the plants and animals you will commonly see as you wander and wonder through the intertidal zone. You will find information about shells, sea lions, anemones, urchins, squids, seaweeds, fishes and so much more. If birds are your passion, many other guides specifically deal with these feathered friends.

Pacific Razor Clam

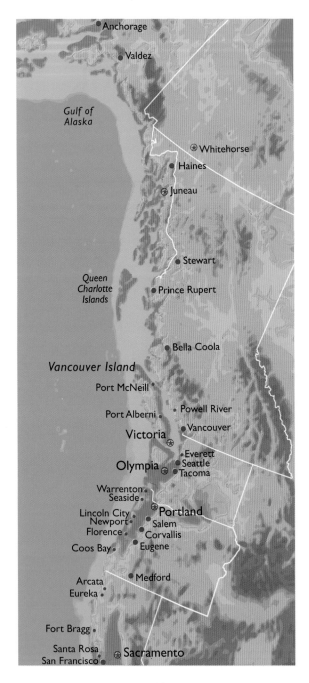

Lurid Rocksnail

How to Use This Guide

At the front (p. 8) is a quick reference guide featuring key species and groups. This reference guide will allow you to make a visual assessment of the object of your interest. Each group is color-coded with a bar to help you find the correct section of the book.

Each species is given a whole page with an illustration or two, text about the plant or animal, and a small text box covering some of the basics, including 'Other Names,' scientific and common, given to the species. First check that the creature resembles the one illustrated. If you are unsure, refer to the inset box and check some of the information given here. 'Range' informs you in which states and provinces it occurs. 'Zone' (described shortly) refers to its position on the shore. 'Habitats' describes the types of places that the creature enjoys, perhaps the tidepools or maybe muddy sand, for example. Dimensions are given so you can determine if the creature is the right size—maximum sizes are given; bear in mind that all things are born small and grow larger.

Ringed Topshell

19

If the animal you are watching is green, but the illustration is red, check 'Color' in the inset box to see if it comes in different colors; many of the creatures you will encounter adapt to their environment, taking on different colors for camouflage. If you are still not satisfied, some entries have a 'Similar Species' category, referring you to other species in the book that look the same. Some similar species are also written about in the main text.

Read all about the object of your fascination in the main text, where you will discover some of the stories behind it and facts about its curious biology. Where possible the use of strange, long scientific words has been avoided. One or two sneak their way in, and there is a glossary at the back (p. 181) if things just don't make sense to you.

The West Coast

The range covered by this guide is chiefly British Columbia, Washington and Oregon. Many of the species will occur beyond these boundaries, and the North American range is described for each entry. Most of the creatures and seaweeds you will encounter in this region thrive in our chilly waters. As you move from north to south, the water gradually gets warmer, and some of the

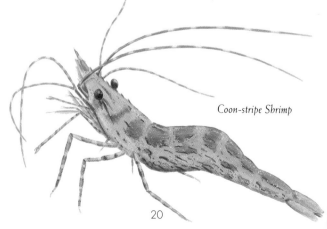

Coon-stripe Shrimp

Stearn's Sea Spider

animals will retreat into the sea to remain cool. Creatures that you commonly find intertidally in the north may never be seen intertidally in the south.

The coastlines of British Columbia and the Northwest are very diverse, from steep cliffs on exposed shores, to the quiet waters of sounds. Some areas are estuarine, where fresh water mixes with salty. Sandy beaches stretch into the distance and look so tempting. If you have ever tried swimming off these beautiful beaches, you know just how cold the water is. The reason for such chilly seas is that the ocean current moves southwards, bringing cold water from the far north.

Tides and the Intertidal Zone

Every coastline is shaped in some way by the tides. Two times a day the tide rises and falls. It seems remarkable that an ocean as enormous as the Pacific can move so much water around. Where does all the water go?

Both the moon and the sun are tugging at the oceans. Just as our planet has the power to attract objects, the moon and the sun do, too. The moon is closer but smaller than the sun. When the moon and sun are aligned, they both tug at the oceans, pulling the water to the side of the planet nearest them. Thus, when the tide rises in one part of the world, it is dropping

Little Rockweed

INTRODUCTION

Tidepool Sculpin

somewhere else. A perfect alignment of the moon and sun creates the greatest rise and fall of the ocean. The most dramatic change in sea level along the West Coast occurs in Puget Sound, with up to 20 feet (6.1 m) between high- and low-tide lines. Just exactly how much the tide will rise and fall depends on the exact position of the sun and moon.

This constant motion of the sea up and down a beach creates distinct zones for wildlife. Near the high-tide line, plants and animals must tolerate long periods out of water, while those at the low-tide line prefer long periods under water. Some creatures and seaweeds are very particular about which part of the beach they will live in. To help you identify an animal or plant, the inset box has an entry for the 'Zone' in which it is found. Several zones are described:

Spray or Splash Zone—the uppermost part of the beach influenced by wave action. Here, the rocks only ever receive splashes from the surf or spray, and are never covered by the sea. (This zone is discussed in the text, not the inset box.)

Upper Intertidal Zone—the uppermost band covered by the highest point of an incoming tide. Here, organisms must tolerate prolonged periods exposed to the elements.

Middle Intertidal Zone—the middle band covered half the time by the tides. More organisms are able to survive here because they are not exposed to drying conditions for too long.

Lower Intertidal Zone—the lowest part of the beach that is only uncovered for a short period of time. Here, growth is luxuriant, because many organisms can tolerate the short exposure to air.

Rough Keyhole Limpet 22

The high-tide line is the highest point that the sea will reach on the incoming tide, and the low-tide line is the point at which the sea is as far out as it will go. Once the tide reaches its lowest point, it begins to come in, or rise, again. Below the low-tide line is the **Subtidal Zone**, never exposed by a receding tide. Here, the life can be very different because it does not have to put up with the rigors of exposure to the air, sun, frosts, rain and beachcombers.

Beachcombing
—What to Do and What Not to Do

There is so much fun to be had from beachcombing, but there are a number of important points to remember to ensure that it is a success and pleasure for you, and for those who come after you.

Choosing the right location is a good start. While all coastlines will have their wildlife, some will be better than others. Gently sloping, rocky beaches riddled with tide-pools are perhaps the most rewarding. But don't count out wading through an Eelgrass meadow, or hiking the fringes of a quiet bay either. Safety is a concern—you don't want to fall off a cliff, be swept away by a large wave, or get stuck in estuarine mud when the tide starts to come in.

Be very wary of the tides, and learn how to read the tide tables that are posted in national parks and at

Penpoint Gunnel

information offices in ports and towns. Tide tables will help you decide what time of day to go to the beach—aim for an ebb tide, because it is safer to follow the water receding out to the low-tide line, than to be chased back up the beach by an advancing tide. Where the shore is very flat the tide can race in, cutting you off on a rocky ledge or sand bar. Be vigilant!

Be aware that some organisms such as the California Mussel (p. 90) thrive where the surf is strongest and waves pound the shores. Freak waves do happen, and they take their victims from time to time. Don't be one of them. It is

very easy to become so engrossed in a tidepool that you lose all sense of time and place, and before you know it, the tide is rushing in with full force. With this caution in mind, beachcombing is best done in a group in case of accidents, and also because your treasured finds are more enjoyable when shared with others.

The treasures of beachcombing come small and large. Bring a pail and a hand lens to study the small creatures. Some of these creatures will only emerge from their homes when under water. A hand lens will help you see the tiny animals that make up a bryozoan colony, for example. And bring this book! It will help you identify and learn about the shore.

Japanese Littleneck

Many people believe that they can take some of their finds home. First, think about where you are—removal is forbidden in many locations. Know the local laws and regulations. Second, think about the luckless victim of your interest. Many sea stars have been transported home in the hope that they will dry and make eye-catching souvenirs. They don't. They rot, they smell bad, and you kill them. Similarly, don't transfer organisms to fresh water—that will kill them too. In short, resist the temptation to take anything home. The rocky tidepool is its home, and it would probably rather stay there.

Many plants and animals of the ocean are considered fine eating. If you are tempted to try them out, never harvest every one in sight. Too many creatures have succumbed to exploitation. It is important to check local regulations regarding sizes of shellfish that are harvested—most have a minimum size requirement to meet before they can

High Cockscomb

be collected. Also, check for information about 'red tide,' which poisons some shellfish, and if you eat them you might well regret it. If you want to harvest some seaweed, don't pull up the whole plant, just trim off part of the plant so that it can still grow and reproduce.

Most important of all, respect the shoreline. It is not yours. You do not own the wildlife on it. Living creatures deserve your love and attention, and try not to interfere. Do turn over rocks to see what is hiding underneath, and do put them back the way you found them, in their original position so the animals feel protected once more. Watch out for creatures as you clamber about the rocks. It is tempting to use mussel and barnacle beds for good footing on steep rocks. Each step you take will kill. A small chip off a mussel shell opens it up to the elements and to predation.

Shield-backed Kelp Crab

Beaches make popular locations for picnics. Make sure you take all your garbage home with you. Plastic waste is hazardous to wildlife and broken glass may end up in the foot of the next beachcomber to follow you. Don't just take your own garbage home with you, but remove what other people have left behind. Sadly, our oceans have long been seen as giant refuse pits, with tons of garbage cast from ships. This garbage floats ashore in its various forms, sometimes dangerous, always ugly.

Shorelife to Discover

The shorelife of the intertidal zone comes in so many shapes and sizes that an overview of each group might help you understand where it fits in with the natural order of things. Some animals look so strange you would be forgiven for thinking that they are plants!

There are animals with backbones (vertebrates), there are animals without backbones (invertebrates) and there are seaweeds (plants). The few vertebrates you will discover are the fishes and mammals, but by far the majority of the creatures you will encounter are invertebrates. The invertebrates covered in this guide fall into distinct groups: mollusks, echinoderms, cnidarians, crustaceans, worms and other small organisms.

Giant Pacific Octopus

Mollusks

The largest group covered by this guide is the mollusks, and it includes some very different organisms indeed. It is hard to believe, but the massive octopus is related to a limpet stuck on a rock. A mollusk is typified by a soft body and a hard shell for protection (though some mollusks have lost this shell). Lining the internal side of the shell is soft tissue called the 'mantle,' and this mantle creates a cavity in which gills for breathing are located. There are distinct groups of mollusks: limpets and snails (the gastropods); bivalves; chitons; sea slugs (the nudibranchs); and squids and octopus (the cephalopods).

Gastropods—limpets and snails—have one large sucking foot and a shell of various forms. The Polyplacophorans—chitons—are limpet-like with their huge

sucking foot, but
they have a line of
eight separate articulat-
ing plates down the back.
The bivalves are all the
clams, oysters and
scallops. They are
grouped together

Leather Star

because they all have two valves, or shells,
which enclose the soft body of the animal,
and a muscular foot often used for burrowing.
The nudibranchs—sea slugs—are also gastropods
but they have lost their shell and rely on other means to
protect themselves. The least likely looking mollusks are
the squids and octopus, called cephalopods. Highly
intelligent and active, they are the most advanced of all the
mollusks.

The dietary preferences of mollusks are as varied as
their forms. Some graze on microscopic algae; some snails
ferociously prey on other snails; squids grapple with lively
prey; and bivalves, filter feeders, suck water into the mantle
cavity to sift it for tiny particles.

Echinoderms

'Echinoderm' means spiny skin, and this group of animals is strictly marine. It includes the sea stars, brittle stars,
sea urchins and sea cucumbers. These are ancient animals
of prehistoric times, and are still very successful today.
They have radial symmetry, usually based on the form of a
five-pointed star. Seawater is pumped around the body to
hydraulically power the tiny tube feet that move the animals around. Their firm structure is given by a calcareous
skeleton most obvious in dead sea urchins, such as the
Eccentric Sand Dollar (p. 114). Echinoderms have the
remarkable ability to regenerate limbs. A spine can regrow
on an urchin, and a whole leg can grow back on a sea
star—however, this ability does not give you license to go
pulling them to pieces!

Cnidarians

Cnidarians are the soft jelly-like animals of the sea.
They include the jellyfish, sea anemones and corals. They
are typified by having stinging tentacles to capture their
prey. The sting comes from tiny cells called nematocysts
lining the tentacles. Corals, of which there is only one in
this guide, are soft-bodied animals that lay down a

calcareous base to
which they attach. It is
the coral 'skeletons' that
make up the elaborate reefs in
tropical waters. Hydroids
resemble extremely small
colonies of corals and occur in
many different forms.

*Fifteen-scaled
Worm*

Crustaceans

These animals have jointed limbs and hard
outer skins, or shells. They are a very successful
group, and are best represented by the crabs. But
shrimps, barnacles and beach fleas are also crustaceans, and
their enormously diverse forms are reflected in the many
different lifestyles and eating habits. Having a tough outer
skeleton has a distinct disadvantage—how do you grow?
Crabs, for example, have overcome this growth problem
by molting periodically. They lose the old, hard skin for a
new, more flexible one that gradually hardens. Molting is a
dangerous time for crustaceans, because their usually tough
outer skin momentarily becomes soft and vulnerable. The
cast-off skeletons frequently wash ashore in great numbers.

Worms

Most of the worms in this guide are annelid worms.
These segmented creatures have many appendages that
assist in walking and breathing. Some wander and are fero-
cious predators, while others, such as Red Tube Worms
(p. 146), stay put, build a tube around themselves, and filter the water with a pretty fan of feather-like appendages
on the head. Another worm featured, the Six-lined
Nemertean (p. 148), is a very different kind of worm not
related to the annelids. Nemerteans do not have distinct
segments, but have one long stretchy body.

Other Small Organisms

There are many other less distinct groups to be found
along the seashore. These groups include the pycnogonids,
bryozoans, poriferans and urochordates.

Pycnogonids are commonly called sea spiders. These
creepy creatures are not related to the true spiders (arach-
nids) that we know so well on land. Only one species of
pycnogonid is represented in this guide.

Bryozoans, sometimes called moss animals, are so
small that they can be missed or mistaken for something

else. Bryozoans are tiny colonial animals that build walled homes of calcium carbonate about them. As the colony expands, it takes on a distinctive form particular to the type of bryozoan. There are many different kinds, and colonies can be shaped like trees, bushes, flat encrustations or grow convincingly as corals. They are filter feeders, using tentacles that extend from their little homes.

Poriferans are simple sponges. They are animals represented by loose aggregations of cells organized to filter water and extract the tiny particles of food from it. Usually, the surface of a sponge is covered in tiny pores through which water passes in and out. Typically, a sponge grows flat in the intertidal zone, but in deeper calmer water it can be much more elaborate and grows to great sizes. Many sponges have tiny silica strands to serve as a skeleton, or support. These small crystals are often used by nudibranchs when they have been ingested.

Urochordates are peculiar animals that actually bear some resemblance and connection to humans—for at least part of their lives. They are classified in the same large group as us, the chordates, but have gone off in their own direction in evolutionary terms. When they are very young and free swimming, they have a nerve cord running down their back, gills and a little tail. They somewhat resemble tadpoles or humans when we are first developing as embryos. Soon all that changes, and what looks like it is going to be an advanced and extraordinary animal, loses all these features, settles down on a rock, and becomes a strange blob of flesh that filters water *Sea Sac* throughout its life. They can be solitary or live in colonies, and are called sea squirts or tunicates.

Seaweeds

The plants of the intertidal zone come in various shapes and sizes, and have been classified accordingly. There are four groups to consider. Algae are divided into three principal groups: brown, green and red. The fourth group, the flowering plants, is only represented by a few grass-like plants in the sea. Collectively, these algae and flowering plants are commonly known as seaweeds.

Algae

The large family of brown algae includes the magnificent kelps. The color is also determined by the dominant pigments for photosynthesis, and they usually come in shades of brown, although some retain rich olive-green colors. The kelps are very successful, forming huge forests just offshore.

Giant Perennial Kelp

The green algae family includes the fleshy green algae of the intertidal zone. The dominant pigments are used to harness the energy from the sun (photosynthesis) and make the algae green. Some are very bright green, while others can be so dark they appear to be black.

Just to confuse the issue of classification, the red algae family can come in shades of red, brown, green or blue. In addition, some have incorporated calcium carbonate into their structures, taking on hard and crusty coralline forms. Some of the red algae can be very beautifully and richly colored, and the exact color they have depends on the balance of the pigments used in photosynthesis.

Flowering Plants

Do not expect to find a sunflower or geranium, but look out for grass-like plants growing in quiet bays or on rocky shores. These are Eelgrass (p. 179) and Surf Grass (p. 178). They are flowering plants like those on land, with a root system and neat rows of inconspicuous flowers tucked in close to the stem. For pollination they rely on the sea to carry pollen from one flower to the next, just in the same way as some grasses rely on the wind.

Surf Grass

Sea Otter
ENHYDRA LUTRIS

Little surpasses the beauty of a playful and intelligent Sea Otter baby nestled on the furry belly of its floating mother. Once persecuted to the point of extinction, the Sea Otter is now making a strong recovery and is a cherished sight for wildlife watchers. A thick pelt, vital for chilly waters, made it a popular animal for trapping. The otter is now protected, and its presence is evidence of a healthy ecosystem. Watch out for the River Otter (*Lutra canadensis*) with its longer tail and slimmer build, because it also takes to the seas.

Five feet (1.5 m) long, and needing copious quantities of fuel to keep warm, the Sea Otter has a voracious appetite for shellfish, crabs, urchins and fish. When the Sea Otter had all but been annihilated, sea urchins grew in such numbers that the kelp forests could not regenerate. With the otter now returning, the kelp forests are healthy and balanced once again. Fisheries still fear the otter's huge appetite, and although protected by law, the Sea Otter is a sad victim of oil spills—the fur's waterproof and insulating qualities are destroyed when oil seeps into it.

RANGE: Alaska, British Columbia, Washington and California, scattered

ZONE: inshore, occasionally on shore

HABITATS: kelp beds

LENGTH: 5 ft (1.5 m)

WEIGHT: 100 lb (45 kg)

Steller Sea Lion

EUMETOPIAS JUBATUS

Hauling themselves out onto the rocky shores, the Steller Sea Lions are mighty mammals that are a treat to see. The massive bulls grow to some 10 feet (3 m) in length and can weigh over 2200 pounds (1000 kg). They somewhat out-size the dainty females, which are a mere third of the bulls' bulk. Such massiveness wins the cows, so watch for the dominant male amidst his harem—he is noticeable also for his thick neck and golden-brown hues. The females are much darker.

OTHER NAME: Northern Sea Lion

RANGE: Alaska to Southern California, scattered

ZONE: intertidal to open water

HABITATS: rocky shores

LENGTH: male to 10 ft (3 m), female to 7 ft (2.1 m)

WEIGHT: male to 2200 lb (1000 kg), female to 800 lb (360 kg)

SIMILAR SPECIES: California Sea Lion (p. 33)

Rather sensitive to people approaching, they will readily dive into the water where they feel safer, and observe you from a distance. Poor weather also drives them in, and long feeding trips to dine on fish may even take them up rivers.

For reasons unknown, the population of this magnificent animal is diminishing. It is thought that competition with humans for certain fish may be the cause—they just cannot compete with our huge nets. This sea lion is larger and lighter in color than the California Sea Lion, the male of which has a prominent ridge on his forehead.

California Sea Lion
ZALOPHUS CALIFORNIANUS

F un-loving performers, the California Sea Lion is bold and sometimes daring. Because of its antics, it is popularly used in marine aquariums to perform tricks and amuse us. In the wild they are just as capable of amusing themselves, and take delight in flinging kelp around and bodysurfing in large waves. Their loud bark can often be heard from afar. Only the males will be seen in the Pacific Northwest, because the females stay at the breeding grounds in Southern California year-round. The males move north after breeding, reaching as far as Vancouver Island.

It is possible to confuse this sea lion with the Steller Sea Lion. The California Sea Lion is darker and smaller, and the male has a prominent ridge on his forehead, a feature lacking in the Steller Sea Lion. The flippers are hairless and black, helping this mammal swim swiftly in the water and dive to the impressive depths of 800 feet (240 m) in its quest for fish and squid. Flat reefs and rocky shores make for great sea lion beach parties, often quite raucous!

RANGE: Southern British Columbia to Southern California

ZONE: intertidal to open water

HABITATS: rocky shores

LENGTH: male to 8 ft (2.4 m), female to 6.5 ft (2 m)

WEIGHT: male to 750 lb (340 kg), female to 250 lb (113 kg)

SIMILAR SPECIES: Steller Sea Lion (p. 32)

Northern Elephant Seal

M I R O U N G A   A N G U S T I R O S T R I S

Aside from beached whales, the Northern Elephant Seal is the largest mammal a beachcomber is likely to encounter. Massively intimidating, these hefty beasts get their name from the extended snout, most especially on the males. During the breeding season it is inflated, appearing larger than usual. The huge males and comparatively tiny females come ashore to breed in California. Males try to impress one another, and frequently scar each other's chest and thickened neck in the process.

RANGE: Alaska to California

ZONE: intertidal, open water

HABITATS: rocky outcrops, offshore

LENGTH: male to 16 ft (4.9 m), female to 9 ft (2.7 m)

WEIGHT: male to 5000 lb (2270 kg), female to 2000 lb (910 kg)

In the Pacific Northwest these seals are sighted during the summer months only. They migrate northwards from their breeding grounds in search of rich feeding and a place to molt. During the molting season they are seen lounging around on rocky shores and islands, seldom doing much at all. Occasional sightings are made in quiet inland waters, but open seas are preferred, and here they can dive to staggering depths of 5000 feet (1500 m) for an hour or more. They feed on fish, squid, octopus and even the occasional shark! Once almost wiped out by over-hunting for their oily skin, they have since made a dramatic recovery.

Pacific Harbor Seal

PHOCA VITULINA

The pretty Harbor Seals are the mammals most likely to be seen in the Pacific Northwest. Found from the open coast into the protected sounds as well as estuaries and up rivers, they are commonly observed. They come in a variety of colors from white to black, the most common combination being a buff color flecked with darker spots.

When the tide is in they are actively diving and hunting, eating all manner of fish. They are partial to the occasional clam or squid. At low tide they haul out onto rocky platforms to sunbathe, where they can be seen singly or in massive groups. The Pacific Harbor Seal will always have one eye open for humans that approach too close. When afraid the seals readily dive into water. Underwater, however, they are in their element, and can be quite curious and friendly with divers. They make themselves unpopular with fishermen, unfortunately, since they cunningly steal fish from nets. They are in turn the prey of Orcas (the killer whales) and even suffer the hungry attentions of the Northern Elephant Seal (p. 34).

OTHER NAME: Leopard Seal

RANGE: Alaska to California

ZONE: intertidal, open water

HABITATS: rocky shores, beaches, sounds, estuaries, rivers

LENGTH: male to 6 ft (1.8 m), female to 5.5 ft (1.7 m)

WEIGHT: male to 300 lb (136 kg), female to 175 lb (79 kg)

High Cockscomb

ANOPLARCHUS PURPURESCENS

Slippery as an eel and as hard to handle, this pretty fish is a common sight under rocks in tidepools and among stones on cobble beaches. When turning rocks you might even find a little gathering of this variably colored fish, which frequently sports two attractive red designer stripes by the eye and a strange crest on its head. Colors may be olive, brown or a stunning rich purple-black that offsets the red fins. Males are particularly fond of brightly colored fins to impress the females. The female is not so brightly colored. Laying as many as 3000 eggs among the rocks, she will wrap herself around the eggs and guard them lovingly until they hatch. Meanwhile, the philandering male abandons her, perhaps for another mate. Both fall prey to garter snakes that wander down to the shore at low tide in search of these tasty morsels.

OTHER NAMES: Cockscomb Prickleback; Crested Blenny

RANGE: Alaska to Southern California

ZONE: lower intertidal, subtidal to 20 ft (6.1 m)

HABITATS: under rocks, tidepools, sheltered coasts, cobble beaches

LENGTH: to 8 in (20 cm)

COLOR: variable

The High Cockscomb is frequently confused with the Slender Cockscomb (*A. insignis*), which, as its name implies, is somewhat thinner and has a smaller crest. Young Monkeyface Pricklebacks (*Cebidichthys violaceus*) lack the spiny texture in the dorsal fin and grow much larger.

Tidepool Sculpin
OLIGOCOTTUS MACULOSUS

When staring into tidepools, you are sure to notice this sculpin. This hardy fish can put up with the rigors of tidepool life, steaming hot one day, bitterly cold the next. Lively characters confined in a small world, they depend on camouflage for protection. The excellent coloration makes them hard to see until they dart about. They are definitely fishes with attitude, and taking the time to watch them is a joy. Perhaps most extraordinary is their ability to return to their home pool—even when taken as much as 330 feet (101 m) away.

Colors are variable, gray-greens being more common. Keep in mind that if the tidepool is predominantly one color, then this scaleless sculpin will match that color. To help blend even further with its habitat, the large fins are almost transparent, with occasional markings. When resting, the dorsal fins fall back flush with the body. Down the back there are sometimes several 'saddles' darker in color. This sculpin is easily confused with the Fluffy Sculpin (*O. snyderi*), which has more hair-like growths on both face and body.

RANGE: Alaska to Southern California

ZONE: middle to upper intertidal

HABITATS: tidepools

LENGTH: to 4 in (10 cm)

COLOR: variable

SIMILAR SPECIES: Smoothhead Sculpin (p. 39)

Penpoint Gunnel
APODICHTHYS FLAVIDUS

Wriggling and writhing like an eel, the Penpoint Gunnel is hard to handle. This strikingly colored fish hides among seaweeds of the intertidal zone. Green, yellow, red or even brown, this fish will take on the colors of its environment—so expect to find a red Penpoint Gunnel in red seaweed. Also hunt for it in tidepools and under rocks. Its name alludes to the long spine at the front of the anal fin along the fish's underside. Other features include the black eye-line and a dark or light line of dots along its flank.

OTHER NAME: Penpoint Blenny

RANGE: Alaska to Southern California

ZONE: middle to lower intertidal

HABITATS: under rocks, Eelgrass beds, tidepools

LENGTH: to 18 in (46 cm)

COLOR: green, yellow, red or brown

Although very common, the fish is seldom seen. A small mouth means it seldom takes a bite on hooked bait, and a slender build saves the fish from being eaten. Crustaceans and mollusks make up its diet. In winter the fish retreat under rocks where they can sometimes be found wrapped tenderly around a white egg mass. The smaller Rockweed Gunnel (*Xererpes fucorum*) lacks the black eye-line, but shares the same habitats. The Crescent Gunnel (*Pholis laeta*) has more elaborate markings with a row of crescents along its back.

Smoothhead Sculpin
A R T E D I U S   L A T E R A L I S

The Smoothhead Sculpin is much larger than the Tidepool Sculpin. Other features that might help you identify this fish apart from the many other confusing species of sculpins include a long, pointed face, large mouth and small eyes set well back. This sculpin is very common in the north of its range where it can be found in tidepools and under rocks. Masterful green and brown coloration can make it very hard to distinguish from its environment. Most of the fins have dark barring and on the upper surfaces the body has scales—these features are lacking in the Tidepool Sculpin.

RANGE: Alaska to Southern California

ZONE: middle to lower intertidal, subtidal to 43 ft (13 m)

HABITATS: tidepools, rocky shores

LENGTH: to 5.5 in (14 cm)

COLOR: green to brown

SIMILAR SPECIES: Tidepool Sculpin (p. 37)

The Smoothhead Sculpin's diet consists of small crustaceans, including shrimps and crabs. Young fish are also consumed, and, much to the annoyance of anglers, they are cunning enough to remove the bait from hooks without being caught themselves. Other signs to look out for include the masses of red eggs tucked away near rocks for protection in tidepools—the eggs are laid in winter, mostly in February.

Rosylip Sculpin

ASCELICHTHYS RHODORUS

Splashes of red adorn the lips and fringe the upper edge of the dorsal fin of the Rosylip Sculpin. Richly colored in olive-browns and cinnamon, it can be a little hard to notice—this sculpin is not so keen to move, preferring to rely on camouflage and stillness for protection. The body is long compared to other sculpins, and it lacks scales, making it very smooth. The dark brown fins have lighter edges. One of the best distinguishing features is the lack of a pelvic fin. In other sculpins, this small fin drops down from the underside like legs. A small cirrus, or hair-like projection, rises on top of the head near the eye.

RANGE: Alaska to Northern California

ZONE: upper to lower intertidal, subtidal to 33 ft (10 m)

HABITATS: tidepools, under rocks, gravel, Eelgrass beds

LENGTH: to 6 in (15 cm)

COLOR: browns

The best places to encounter this pretty face are in tidepools, where they are abundant, and under rocks at low tide. Gravel beaches and dense Eelgrass beds are also favored. This sculpin can be very common in some parts of its range. The Rosylip Sculpin seldom seizes baited hooks, and if it did, it would surely just anger anglers, because its small size makes it worthless for eating.

Flathead Clingfish

GOBIESOX MAEANDRICUS

An oversized tadpole best describes this intertidal fish. The broad, flattened head and narrow, tapered body are very distinctive. Specially modified fins on the underside of the head allow the tenacious clingfish to suck onto the underside of rocks in shallow water. Lift a rock gently and look at the underside to see if clingfishes are hanging on for their lives. The sucking disc on the underside is so successful that it can be a challenge to remove the fish. If you succeed, place it on the palm of your hand and hold it upside down—they really do cling!

The clingfish can also be found under kelp. It forages on other under-rock inhabitants, especially small crustaceans, mollusks and worms. The female lays a clutch of eggs on the underside of a rock and the male will guard the eggs until they hatch. The color of a clingfish is variable, from light and dark browns and reds, with mottling and a pale bridge usually connecting the eyes. These fish are common but frequently overlooked because of their habit of hiding under rocks and their dark colors.

OTHER NAME: Northern Clingfish

RANGE: Alaska to Southern California

ZONE: intertidal and subtidal to 26 ft (7.9 m)

HABITATS: under rocks and kelp

LENGTH: to 6 in (15 cm)

COLOR: variable red and brown, mottled

Grunt Sculpin

RHAMPHOCOTTUS RICHARDSONII

Undeniably the most adorable of our intertidal fish, the Grunt Sculpin deserves a place in our hearts for its comical shape and strange behavior. To add to its peculiarity, when it is removed from the water, strange wheezing-grunting sounds can be heard—clearly a protest to be returned to the water! Quite boxy in shape, it is obviously not designed for streamlined athleticism, and instead moves about the bottom in short jerks and jumps, propelled by the longer rays at the bottom of its pectoral fins.

RANGE: Alaska to Washington
ZONE: lower intertidal to subtidal
HABITATS: tidepools, rocky shores, pilings, sand bottoms
LENGTH: to 3.25 in (8.3 cm)
COLOR: cream, brown and red

The Grunt has a pale cream base color, marked with brownish streaks and a bright red patch at the base of the tail. The two eyes move independently of each other, weirdly scanning for small edible crustaceans that it will peck off with its snout-like mouth. Some Grunt Sculpins will take up residence in the empty shells of Giant Acorn Barnacles (p. 136) or other convenient niches such as bottles or other garbage. In the breeding season the female has the upper hand, pursuing the male until he is trapped in a recess in which he is confined until she lays her eggs for him to fertilize.

Sand Sole

PSETTICHTHYS MELANOSTICTUS

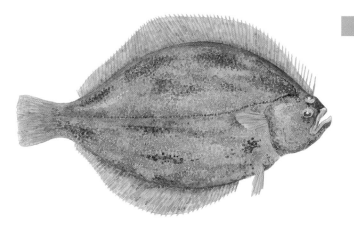

This flatfish is sometimes stranded in sandy tidepools. You would be forgiven for thinking that there is nothing in the empty-looking tidepool, but look again. The Sand Sole not only matches the color of the sand so well, but it also flaps its fins and partially buries itself. Older, larger Sand Soles will seldom be found in these pools.

The Sand Sole is different from other flatfish or flounders in that the first several sharp rays on the dorsal fin have no membrane between them. This is a right-eyed fish, so that the upper surface is always the right-hand side of the fish. Try to think of flatfish as tall, thin fishes that decided to flop over on one side, and so had to move an eye over to the other side of their faces. The upper surface is colored, while the underside is pale. The Sand Sole is frequently caught by inshore anglers and makes for fine dining, which gives it some market value. Fortunately for the Sand Sole, its preference for shallow waters protects it from large-scale commercial fisheries.

RANGE: Alaska to Southern California

ZONE: inshore and subtidal to 600 ft (183 m)

HABITATS: sandy tidepools, sandy bottoms

LENGTH: to 24.5 in (62.2 cm)

COLOR: black-speckled tan, brown

Black Prickleback
XIPHISTER ATROPURPUREUS

Chocolate-brown or black, this lithe eel-like fish has some distinctive markings on the face that help us to identify it. Two comical, black bands descend from the eye and are bordered in white. The similar Rock Prickleback (*X. mucosus*) has eye bands that are pale and bordered in black. At the base of the tail, most Black Pricklebacks have a white band. The pectoral fin just behind the gills is so small as to be hardly noticeable.

OTHER NAME: Black Blenny

RANGE: Alaska to Southern California

ZONE: lower intertidal, subtidal to 25 ft (7.6 m)

HABITATS: tidepools, under rocks, rocky shores

LENGTH: to 12 in (30 cm)

COLOR: dark red-brown to black

Black Pricklebacks are common fish when the tide is out. Larger ones will tend to hide under rocks, while the younger, smaller pricklebacks can be seen in tidepools. Be careful when turning rocks because there may be several males underneath, all wrapped around their egg masses. They patiently wait up to three weeks for the eggs to hatch. Be especially careful when placing the rock back where it was. Some land animals such as garter snakes and feisty minks will come down at low tide to dine on sheltering pricklebacks.

44

White-cap Limpet

ACMAEA MITRA

The White-cap Limpet is frequently washed up on shores, where the strong surf has pounded the shell to a dull white. Unlike other limpets, with their low profile, the shell of this limpet is very high compared to its length, giving it a pronounced cone-shaped appearance. The base is almost round, and the apex, or high point of the shell, quite central. The shell is thick and the interior a smooth white.

When alive, the White-cap Limpet is more likely to appear pink, because it is encrusted with Encrusting Coral (p. 177) on which it feeds. Found on exposed rocky shores as well as protected rocky areas, its high and prominent shell would be a disadvantage in rough surf, but a powerful foot keeps it well adhered to the rock. Look out for this limpet at low tide, and do not confuse it with its smaller cousin, the Corded White Limpet (A. funiculata), which shows ribs radiating from the central apex.

OTHER NAME: Dunce-cap Limpet

RANGE: Alaska to Southern California

ZONE: lower intertidal, subtidal to 100 ft (30 m)

HABITATS: exposed and protected rocky shores

LENGTH: to 1.5 in (3.8 cm)

HEIGHT: to 1 in (2.5 cm)

COLOR: white shell, pink growths

45

Fingered Limpet
LOTTIA DIGITALIS

When you clamber about on the rocks high up the beach, there are few animals to be noticed. One of the conspicuous mollusks to be found is the Fingered Limpet. Closely hugging rocks, this oval shell is colored gray-green and brown, with paler spots flecked here and there. Strong ribs radiate outwards from the apex (high point) of the shell, making the edge of shell wavy. The slightly hooked apex is close to the front end of the shell.

OTHER NAMES: Ribbed Limpet; *Collisella digitalis*

RANGE: Alaska to Southern California

ZONE: upper intertidal and splash zone

HABITATS: exposed rocky shores

LENGTH: to 1.25 in (3.18 cm)

COLOR: gray-green, brown, white spots

This tolerant limpet enjoys the pounding surf but avoids the baking sun of the high intertidal zone where it grazes on algae. Vertical surfaces facing the surf are preferred, and crevices offer a bit of protection. A powerful foot sucks firmly onto the rock—a great deal of force is needed to remove a limpet, so leave them alone because you risk damaging their shells. Empty limpet shells reveal a glossy white or pale blue interior with a rich caramel-colored blotch at the high point. A black wavy margin adds to its beauty.

File Limpet
LOTTIA LIMATULA

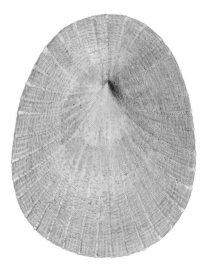

Tiny beads or scales compressed into fine ribs give this limpet its name. Its fine-woven texture will often give the creature a serrated edge, although it sometimes wears away. Tan to greenish-brown above, the interior is white with a dark rim and a small brown spot in the middle. The apex (high point) is set towards the front end of the shell, and the profile is very low, so that the limpet hugs the rocks closely.

The File Limpet becomes more common in the southern parts of its range, but it does occur as far north as Puget Sound. It grazes on microscopic algae covering the rocks, and each limpet has its own preferred feeding grounds to which it likes to return.

OTHER NAME: *Collisella limatula*

RANGE: Washington to Southern California

ZONE: middle to lower intertidal

HABITATS: exposed and protected rocky shores

LENGTH: to 1.75 in (4.4 cm)

COLOR: tan to greenish-brown

Limpets will take on different proportions depending on where they choose to live. Study a large rock with limpets on both sides, and you will notice how the limpets on the sheltered side grow taller and more elaborately than those on the wave-swept side where a low profile is more important.

Rough Keyhole Limpet

DIODORA ASPERA

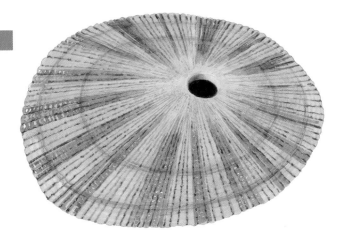

Rather like a volcano with a crater at its summit, this limpet is an attractive find at the low-tide line. The hole at the apex (high point) allows the limpet to send a current of water over its gills, the water shooting out of the top. The base is oval in shape and often fringed with small 'teeth' because of the many fine ribs radiating from the apex. The color is variable, from gray to white with dark gray or purple rays. The underside is plain white. It is not so selective about its diet: algae, encrusting sponges and bryozoans will do just fine.

RANGE: Alaska to Southern California

ZONE: lower intertidal, subtidal to 50 ft (15 m)

HABITATS: rocky shores

LENGTH: to 2.75 in (7 cm)

COLOR: white or gray with darker rays

Hidden away between the mantle and the foot is the surprisingly large worm, *Arctonoe vittata*. This commensal relationship benefits both parties. The worm gets a protective home and reportedly, as a rental payment perhaps, will protect the limpet from marauding sea stars—the worm nips the feet of attacking sea stars to put them off. If this fails, the limpet will extend its mantle over the rough shell, thus becoming slippery smooth and impossible for the sea stars to grasp.

Mask Limpet
TECTURA PERSONA

This abundant limpet is not as conspicuous as the Fingered Limpet (p. 46). Search in wave-washed crevices near the high-tide line or round the base of boulders. In protected bays they can be more obvious. The shell is elliptical, slightly narrower at one end, and rises to quite a height, giving it a deep profile. It is mostly a gray-brown on the upper side, but there can be tints of blue, and numerous white bars might be dense enough to give it a checkered look.

The Mask Limpet, like most limpets, is a grazer, slowly moving about the rocks chipping away at the surface with its finely serrated radula (tongue).

OTHER NAMES: Speckled Limpet; *Notoacmaea persona*

RANGE: Alaska to Northern California

ZONE: upper intertidal

HABITATS: exposed, protected rocky shores, crevices

LENGTH: to 2 in (5 cm)

COLOR: gray-brown, white markings

SIMILAR SPECIES: Pacific Plate Limpet (p. 50)

Feeding takes place mostly in the dark, and preferably on the ebb tide when there are fresh deposits left behind. Empty shells reveal a pale blue-white and highly polished interior. The underside has a dark brown margin and an irregular brown spot that sometimes takes on the form of a face, thereby giving this limpet its name. Be sure to compare your find with the similar Pacific Plate Limpet.

Pacific Plate Limpet

TECTURA SCUTUM

The Pacific Plate Limpet rather resembles the Mask Limpet, but is not so high. So comparatively flat it is that it got named after dinnerware. Smoothly textured, the upper side is a gentle brown or green-brown in color, and beautifully marked with cream-colored lines radiating from the apex. Sometimes this limpet can be seen transporting a rooftop garden of strands of algae all gently waving in the current.

OTHER NAME: *Notoacmaea scutum*

RANGE: Alaska to Northern California

ZONE: middle to lower intertidal, subtidal

HABITATS: rocky shores

LENGTH: to 2.5 in (6.4 cm)

COLOR: brown, green-brown, cream markings

SIMILAR SPECIES: Mask Limpet (p. 49)

This limpet moves up and down with the tide, consuming microscopic and encrusting algae. It is nocturnal by nature, and can be seen tightly huddled against rocks by day. The smell of a starfish is enough to make this limpet break into a run, though remember that speed is all relative, and a limpet running and panting still looks painfully slow. Should it succumb to the starfish's pursuit, then the empty shell is a pretty one to find. A glossy white underside is bordered with an intermittent dark brown band, with additional splotches of brown in the middle.

Japanese Abalone
HALIOTIS KAMTSCHATKANA

These unusual mollusks are much prized for their firm flesh. They can be hard to come by in the intertidal zone because many have been collected. Fortunately for the Japanese Abalone, the oval shell is frequently encrusted with algae, helping it to blend in with its environment and avoid detection. Sucked onto rocks like a limpet, the abalone gently moves about grazing on the thin film of algae. Please do not remove them out of curiosity, because their thin shells can be damaged easily, which leaves them vulnerable to predators such as starfish.

OTHER NAME: Pinto Abalone

RANGE: Alaska to Northern California

ZONE: lower intertidal, subtidal to 115 ft (35 m)

HABITATS: rocks, kelp

LENGTH: to 7 in (18 cm)

COLOR: red-brown, iridescent inside

The shell is thickened to one side and rather rough in texture. The color is usually brown, with tints of red or pink, and a line of holes along the outer edge. These holes act in the same way as the hole of the Rough Keyhole Limpet (p. 48), allowing a current of water to pass through the shell. Only a few of the new, outermost holes will be open. Empty shells reveal a dazzling array of colors from iridescent blues, greens and yellows on white.

Frilled Dogwinkle
NUCELLA LAMELLOSA

The Frilled Dogwinkle, in shades of yellow, white and pale brown, has decorations that are determined by its environment. If you are hunting for snails on the exposed coasts where surf is strong, then look for smooth shells. In quieter waters, frills develop rather elaborately, because there is no rough water to make this a disadvantage—it would be hard for a snail to look after frilly appendages in rough seas. This dogwinkle is found in crevices among rocks. Look under rocks near the low-tide line for clusters of yellowish eggs.

OTHER NAME: Wrinkled Purple

RANGE: Alaska to Northern California

ZONE: middle intertidal to shallow subtidal

HABITATS: rocky shores

LENGTH: to 4 in (10 cm)

COLOR: brown, green-brown, cream markings

SIMILAR SPECIES: Leafy Thorn Purpura (p. 60)

This dogwinkle is a carnivore, feasting on barnacles and mussels, clams and oysters. So effective and common is it that, in some regions, the lower spread of the Acorn Barnacle (p. 135) and the upper limit of mussels are determined by this snail's appetite. In turn this gastropod is consumed by the Red Crab (p. 127). When threatened, or to hide from the weather and the sun when the tide is out, the snail withdraws into its shell and tightly closes the door, its 'operculum.'

Emarginate Dogwinkle
NUCELLA EMARGINATA

Sometimes pretty, sometimes dull, this highly variable species is a resident of exposed rocky shores, often among the crevices near barnacle and mussel beds. It feeds on both of these, drilling a neat hole in the shell. Of the mussels, it prefers the Blue Mussel (p. 91), perhaps because the shell is thinner and requires less work. This dogwinkle also lives on shores that are slightly protected, but is absent from quiet water.

The snail is stubby, with a short spire, and its ribs are often white and set against a dark colored base, giving a striped appearance. Colors vary from yellow to dark brown and gray. The opening to the shell is tinted yellow, and if the snail is still inside, a dark brown operculum (door) will be tightly shut against you. The operculum also protects against water loss when the tide is out. When the Emarginate Dogwinkle is dull-colored, it could be confused with the Channeled Dogwinkle, but usually where one occurs the other is absent. Hermit crabs enjoy taking up residence in these small and manageable homes when the snail inside has died.

OTHER NAME: Striped Dogwinkle

RANGE: Alaska to Southern California

ZONE: middle to lower intertidal

HABITATS: rocky shores

LENGTH: to 1 in (2.5 cm)

COLOR: variable, yellow, brown gray, white stripes

SIMILAR SPECIES: Channeled Dogwinkle (p. 54)

Channeled Dogwinkle

NUCELLA CANALICULATA

The Channeled Dogwinkle is a pale, mostly white or gray snail with a hint of yellow or tan inside the opening of the shell. The prominent ribs are set above deep ridges that may also be tinted with some tan coloration. This dogwinkle is less common in British Columbia than in Oregon or Washington, and it prefers a rocky environment where barnacles and mussels abound. This is a carnivore, and it has a special mouth-part that allows it to drill through the seemingly impenetrable barnacle shells. It might take a good day or two for the Channeled Dogwinkle to consume a barnacle.

RANGE: Alaska to Northern California

ZONE: middle to lower intertidal, subtidal

HABITATS: rocky shores

LENGTH: to 1.5 in (3.8 cm)

COLOR: white-gray, tan

SIMILAR SPECIES: Emarginate Dogwinkle (p. 53)

While it is slimmer than many dogwinkles, throughout its range this mollusk can be confused with the very similar File Dogwinkle (*N. lima*) that has many ribs closely set to one another. Its shell is somewhat shorter and fatter than the Channeled Dogwinkle, and it hides in the rocky crevices where it is protected from the surf.

Dire Whelk
SEARLISIA DIRA

The dismal gray version of this elegant snail might have inspired such a bad name, but it does come in more attractive and variable shades of brown. The aperture, or opening, to the shell is a chocolate-brown. Found on rocky shores and frequently in tidepools, the shell sometimes sports a pink or white coating of encrusting algae. The twisting spire is long, with many ribs that sculpt the lip of the aperture where the shell is quite thin.

Presence of this whelk is certainly dire news for many of the residents of tidepools and the rocky shores. It is both scavenger and carnivore, and will feast on living limpets, chitons and other snails. Injured animals will have to suffer the attentions of the whelk as well, because it will start biting at any part that it can. The Dire Whelk will also exploit feeding starfish, chewing on the prey it is holding onto. Carrion will do just fine as well, the whelks homing in on anything they can smell—something for which they have quite a talent.

OTHER NAME: Spindle Whelk

RANGE: Alaska to Northern California

ZONE: middle to lower intertidal

HABITATS: rocky shores, open coast, bays

LENGTH: to 2 in (5 cm)

COLOR: gray to brown

SIMILAR SPECIES: Lurid Rocksnail (p. 57)

Sculptured Rocksnail

OCENEBRA INTERFOSSA

This little carnivore comes in many shapes, but only grows to 0.75 inches (1.9 cm). Some have whorls that are very distinct and prominently ridged, while others, as illustrated, are smoother. Deep grooves are interspersed between the ribs. The color varies from gray to orange-brown and the surface texture is usually a rough one. Barnacles, oysters and clams make up its diet. It drills a hole with its radula, a serrated tongue, and then proceeds to dine on the flesh inside. There's not much a barnacle can do about it, because it is firmly stuck to the rock and unable to run away from this rocksnail. Rocky shores and quieter waters are the domain of this gastropod.

The Lurid Rocksnail occurs with the Sculptured Rocksnail, but has a smoother shell. The Atlantic Oyster Drill (*Urosalpinx cinerea*) is the same size but with less ridging and is colored yellow-gray. Introduced from the east, the Oyster Drill is commonly found in the oyster farms of the Northwest, and gets little respect from the farmers.

OTHER NAMES: Carpenter's Dwarf Triton; *Ocinebrina interfossa*

RANGE: Alaska to Southern California

ZONE: middle to lower intertidal, subtidal to 20 ft (6.1 m)

HABITATS: sheltered rocky shores

LENGTH: to 0.75 in (1.9 cm)

COLOR: variable gray to orange-brown

SIMILAR SPECIES: Lurid Rocksnail (p. 57)

Lurid Rocksnail

OCENEBRA LURIDA

Only growing to 1.5 inches (3.8 cm), this mollusk is beautifully formed with well-rounded whorls. The Lurid Rocksnail prefers rocky or gravelly shores near the low-tide line or in subtidal waters. However, in the more southerly part of its range, it becomes a subtidal species, preferring the cool of the water. Around the whorls are numerous ribs that are variably pronounced from snail to snail. The pale yellows, caramels and browns are sometimes overlaid with darker streaking. Barnacles are the mainstay of its diet, the snails drilling through the tough shell of the crustaceans to consume them from within their protective homes. Some have been seen to rasp away at the almighty Gumboot Chiton (p. 92), which could feed a rocksnail for life!

The Lurid Rocksnail can be easily confused with the Columbian Amphissa (*Amphissa columbiana*). The latter is more slender and has a longer aperture than the rounded, oval features of the Lurid Rocksnail. The rocksnail may also be mistaken for the Dire Whelk, which is grayer in coloration and has a longer, less-rounded spire.

OTHER NAMES: Lurid Dwarf Triton; *Ocinebrina lurida*

RANGE: Alaska to Northern California

ZONE: lower intertidal, subtidal to 180 ft (55 m)

HABITATS: rocky shores

LENGTH: to 1.5 in (3.8 cm)

COLOR: variable pale yellow, brown

SIMILAR SPECIES: Sculptured Rocksnail (p. 56), Dire Whelk (p. 55)

Carinate Dove Shell
ALIA CARINATA

Carinate Dove Shells are so small, but they are such a delight to inspect closely. Found along most of the West Coast, the best place to hunt for them is in grass beds and on kelps—look along the low-tide line. The shell patterns are very variable, usually being composed of caramels and browns over a cream background. Colored bands sometimes follow the twists of the long spire. The last whorl ends in a pronounced lip richly colored in dark browns. On living snails, look for the white foot flecked with black. They are very active for their size, compared to many of the other snails.

OTHER NAMES: Keeled Dove Shell; *Mitrella carinata*

RANGE: Alaska to Southern California

ZONE: lower intertidal, subtidal to 15 ft (4.6 m)

HABITATS: kelp, Eelgrass beds, algae

LENGTH: 0.4 in (1 cm)

COLOR: variable cream, caramel, brown

This snail is thought to graze the surface of algae and kelp for all the other much smaller, even microscopic, organisms that reside there. Abandoned shells are a popular choice among young hermit crabs looking for a small but luxurious residence, before growing and moving on to something larger. Barely growing to half an inch (1.27 cm), these snails are ideal for young hermit crabs, but they are easy for us to miss.

Oregon Triton
FUSITRITON OREGONENSIS

One of our largest gastropod snails, the Oregon Triton grows to as much as 6 inches (15 cm) in length. This snail is common at and below the low-tide line, and it enjoys rocky areas. The pale shell is covered in a tough brown periostracum that forms all the unusual hairy projections, which can wear off in rough conditions and as the snail ages. Hairs are lined spirally and cross vertical ribs, giving a checkered appearance.

OTHER NAME: Hairy Oregon Triton

RANGE: Alaska to Southern California

ZONE: low-tide line, subtidal to 400 ft (120 m)

HABITATS: sand, rubble

LENGTH: to 6 in (15 cm)

COLOR: brown

An aggressive predator, the triton has a rare and peculiar preference for sea urchins at which they peck away. Living sea urchins bearing small black scars are the evidence to its foraging. Tunicates are also eaten. Males can be somewhat possessive about their mates, hitching a ride on a female's back and fending off other males. Egg cases, resembling ears of corn, are laid in distinctive coils. When juveniles hatch from the eggs, the first thing they do is eat each other. The remaining few go on to become the elegant and familiar Oregon Tritons.

Leafy Thorn Purpura

CERATOSTOMA FOLIATUM

Finely frilled and delicately colored, this snail's beauty is sufficient to rival some of the more stunning tropical species. Three frills run vertically up the spire, and their elaborateness depends on where the snail lives. On the exposed coast where the snail tolerates surging currents, large frills would be a disadvantage. Where the water is calmer, the snail can grow frills to its heart's content. White in color, the shell is often adorned with attractive bands of reddish-browns—the same color as the horny operculum shutting the snail inside. Farther north the snails show more darker coloration.

OTHER NAME: Leafy Hornmouth

RANGE: Alaska to Southern California

ZONE: lower intertidal, subtidal to 200 ft (61 m)

HABITATS: rocky shores, boulders, tidepools

LENGTH: to 3.5 inches (8.9 cm)

COLOR: white, yellow with dark bands

The frills have an interesting function beyond looks. Fish dislodge snails so that when they fall, they land with the aperture facing up. The fish has easy access to the foot and a tasty morsel. This snail, however, has a much higher chance of landing the right way up, flicked by the currents generated by the frills as it falls. Barnacles and bivalves make up its diet, and in late winter it lays yellow egg cases, frequently on its own shell.

Mudflat Snail
BATILLARIA ATTRAMENTARIA

Small and copious, this snail with its spire will be noticed if you are wandering the mudflats of quiet bays. One of the many illegal ecological immigrants of the past, this snail hitched a ride with Japanese oysters earlier in the 20th century. It seems rather happy on the West Coast. It is hardy and very tolerant of low salinity, such as in estuaries, and cold temperatures. In the quiet waters many tiny particles settle on the surface of the mud, and with each tide there is a new deposit. It is on these particles that the tiny snails graze.

OTHER NAMES: False-cerith Snail; *B. cumingi*; *B. zonalis*

RANGE: British Columbia to California

ZONE: upper to middle intertidal

HABITATS: sand, mud, quiet water, salt marsh

HEIGHT: 1.5 in (3.8 cm)

COLOR: gray-brown

SIMILAR SPECIES: Giant Pacific Bittium (p. 62)

The tall spire is gray-brown with variable darker markings. The last whorl ends with a well-rounded aperture. The operculum inside seals off the mollusk so well it can survive for two weeks without fresh water! Look closely at the operculum and growth lines will be evident, showing how it has grown bigger as the snail has grown. This slender snail is similar in design and color to the Giant Pacific Bittium, but the latter is smaller and has a glossy appearance.

Giant Pacific Bittium

BITTIUM ESCHRICHTII

The Giant Pacific Bittium only grows to 0.75 inches (1.9 cm), and is only a 'giant' when compared to its close cousins in the same genus—they are smaller still. This tall, thin snail is common under rocks in the intertidal zone, and can also be observed feeding on Eelgrass (p. 179) or encrusting algae in tidepools. This snail is a generalist for little chunks of any alga that it can swallow or chew on.

The elegant spire is gray to reddish-brown and marked with darker grooves that twist around the spire. The smooth texture gives a slightly shiny appearance and the oval aperture has a sharp lip. Most similar in appearance is the Mudflat Snail but there are a number of differences. The shape of the aperture of the Mudflat Snail is very round, it grows to a greater length, and it lacks the dark grooves of the Giant Pacific Bittium. Empty Bittium shells are a favorite for tiny hermit crabs—perhaps the long thin shape is easy to haul around on a hermit's back.

OTHER NAME: Threaded Horn Snail

RANGE: Alaska to Southern California

ZONE: intertidal, subtidal to 180 ft (55 m)

HABITATS: under rocks, Eelgrass beds, tidepools, oyster beds

HEIGHT: 0.75 in (1.9 cm)

COLOR: brown, green-brown, cream markings

SIMILAR SPECIES: Mudflat Snail (p. 61)

Tinted Wentletrap

EPITONIUM TINCTUM

Exquisitely sculptured, the Tinted Wentletrap is a tiny treasure. Its unusual name comes from the Danish word for a spiral staircase, inspired by the 8 to 14 white ribs running the length of the shell. These ribs are offset against a gently colored shell tinted in brown and purple. The round aperture has a thick white lip, and is closed by a horny operculum when the snail is alive.

These dainty snails rarely wander far from their food sources—the Aggregating and Giant Green anemones (pp. 121 and 122). Often buried in sand nearby, they emerge to peck out chunks of the anemone's tentacles and foot. Tinted Wentletraps gather in small groups, and when exposed by an ebb tide, burrow and conceal themselves in soft sand. If you notice a wentletrap moving about at speed and in an irregular fashion, you are more likely observing the antics of the Hairy Hermit Crab (p. 134), the young of which are rather fond of these shells. The Money Wentletrap (*E. indianorum*) looks similar, but it is all white, larger at 1.5 inches (3.8 cm), and lives in deeper waters.

OTHER NAME: Painted Wentletrap

RANGE: British Columbia to Southern California

ZONE: low-tide line, subtidal to 150 ft (46 m)

HABITATS: near anemones

HEIGHT: 0.6 in (1.5 cm)

COLOR: tinted white, white ribs

Ringed Topshell
CALLIOSTOMA ANNULATUM

This ocean jewel is a rare treat of the intertidal zone, and it is found more commonly in the north of its range. Preferring to live in subtidal kelp forests, it can occasionally be found near shore. It is unique in that it has a yellow shell with a band of pink or purple, and spirals of purplish beads winding their way round the sharply conical shell. The body of the snail, which is salmon-pink and flecked with brown, adds even more jazzy colors. Unfortunately all these brilliant colors will fade a little when the mollusk dies.

OTHER NAME: Purple-ringed Topshell

RANGE: Alaska to Southern California

ZONE: lower intertidal, subtidal to 100 ft (30 m)

HABITATS: kelp forests, rocky shores, open coast

HEIGHT: to 1.25 in (3.1 cm)

COLOR: pink-purple on yellow

This snail has omnivorous eating habits. Kelp makes up part of its diet, as does almost anything else that is growing on the kelp. On the seafloor, it pursues many of the smaller animals. When attacking, the Ringed Topshell rears up on its foot spreading it wide, then lunges at the target and traps it. Carrion makes good eating, too, and this snail has a keen nose for it.

Western Ribbed Topshell

CALLIOSTOMA LIGATUM

As tempting as a colorful candy, this beautiful top-shell is caramel-brown and wrapped with tan spiral ridges, giving a striped appearance. Compared to other topshells such as the flat-sided Ringed Topshell (p. 64), its appearance is chubby from the rounded whorls. Where the shell is older and worn, a delicate nacreous (pearly) blue shines through, giving this topshell its other name. The muscular foot of the mollusk is black with orange or creamy patches. This topshell is a common find under rocks and in crevices of the intertidal zone along protected rocky shores, and it can also be found to con-siderable depths.

OTHER NAME: Blue Topsnail
RANGE: Alaska to California
ZONE: middle to lower inter-tidal, subtidal to 100 ft (30 m)
HABITATS: rocky shores
HEIGHT: to 1 in (2.5 cm)
COLOR: brown, tan stripes

Something of a non-fussy eater, this topshell will graze on kelp and algae, and quite enjoys the occasional sponge or tunicate. The sight or smell of a starfish is enough to send this snail running. If it is not fast enough, it will cover itself with a mucus coating. This slippery goo makes it rather difficult for the predatory starfish to grasp the shell with its tube feet, and on a lucky day the snail might just slip out of its grasp.

Red Turban

ASTRAEA GIBBEROSA

This impressive, sturdy snail's shell comes in brick reds and browns. The heavy brown periostracum covers a knobbly shell, giving the snail a rough texture. Beneath this surface layer the shell is stunningly nacreous, the colors of which are hinted at in the aperture of the shell. The snail shuts itself inside with a thick, smooth operculum. Aboriginals used the whitish oval operculum for personal ornamentation and for in-lay work.

In the southern part of its range the Red Turban prefers deeper water, and is seldom seen in Oregon and Washington. It is a locally abundant mollusk, especially in British Columbia, and favors rocky beaches, either sheltered or open. Look among the rocks at low tide. The Red Turban can also be found subtidally to considerable depths. The upper surface of the shell is sometimes smothered in patches of encrusting algae, helping the snail to blend in with the rocks around it. Despite looking so tough and impenetrable, the Red Turban falls victim to sea stars.

RANGE: British Columbia to Southern California

ZONE: lower intertidal, subtidal to 270 ft (82 m)

HABITATS: rocky shores, open or quiet coasts

HEIGHT: to 2.25 in (5.7 cm)

WIDTH: to 3 in (7.6 cm)

COLOR: reddish-brown

Dusky Tegula
TEGULA PULLIGO

Less abundant than the Black Tegula (p. 68), but still quite common in the north of its range, the Dusky Tegula is a shell of the intertidal zone and the shallow subtidal waters. Young Duskies can be found on rocks, while the adults are more often found on kelp. Rocky shores along the open coast are preferred.

About 1.5 inches (3.8 cm) high, the Dusky Tegula is a little wider than it is high. The shell is sharply conical and rather flat-sided. Mostly brown, the true colors of the shell are often obscured by an encrusting growth of algae. The brown is flecked with lighter markings, especially below the suture of the whorls, and is sometimes tinted with purple. Some shells come much darker than others, lacking the orange hue. The shell has a very flat bottom with paler colors, and the interior is pearly white. When the snail is still resident, it shuts itself away using a round operculum (door) until the next tide comes in. When crawling about, the colorful foot can be seen. It is mostly black with a reddish-brown border and fringes of pink near the head.

OTHER NAME: Northern Brown Turban

RANGE: Alaska to Southern California

ZONE: middle to lower intertidal, subtidal to 10 ft (3 m)

HABITATS: rocky shores

HEIGHT: to 1.5 in (3.8 cm)

COLOR: variable browns

Black Tegula
TEGULA FUNEBRALIS

Abundant snails of the West Coast, these tegulas enjoy the harsh high intertidal reaches of rocky shores along open coasts. Smaller individuals tend to be higher up the shore than the larger individuals, and large aggregations collect in sheltered crevices when the tide is out. The Black Tegula is a herbivore, grazing on the thin film of algae on rocks as well as larger pieces of vegetable matter.

OTHER NAME: Black Turban
RANGE: Alaska to Northern California
ZONE: upper to lower intertidal
HABITATS: rocky shores, open coast
HEIGHT: to 1.75 in (4.4 cm)
COLOR: black, blue-black

Mostly black or blue-black, the summit of the spire erodes to reveal the shiny pearl surface beneath. Many tegulas will have a hitchhiker or two, including the Black Limpet (*Lottia asmi*) and the Slipper Snail (*Crepidula adunca*), which resembles a limpet. The Black Limpet grazes on algae on the shell's surface, and will hop onto a new ride when the snails collect together in a group. The Slipper Snail, with its hooked apex, just seems to enjoy the ride, filtering the water from on high. Red Crabs (p. 127) and Ochre Sea Stars (p. 111) love to dine on Black Tegulas.

Dall's Dwarf Turban
HOMALOPOMA LURIDUM

Like tiny pebbles, Dall's Dwarf Turbans are easy to overlook. These residents of the open and protected rocky coasts are tucked under rocks at the low-tide line and the shallow waters. More abundant in the north of its range, in Oregon, the diminutive Berry Dwarf Turban (*H. baculum*) may be more noticeable, although it only grows to 0.2 inches (0.5 cm) and lacks the ribs of Dall's Dwarf Turban.

The almost round shell comes in variable dull hues of gray, red and purple. The shell is very thick for its size, and the aperture is small with a thick lip. Most of the shell is made up of the last whorl, the body whorl, and the ridges are quite obvious. Three or four whorls form the blunt spire. The shell can be confused with the Tucked Lirularia, but this equally small snail has a thinner shell and less-distinct ribbing. In addition, the operculum (door) of Dall's Dwarf Turban is very thick compared to the Lirularia. Abandoned shells make ideal homes for the youngest of hermit crabs.

OTHER NAME: Dark Dwarf Turban

RANGE: Alaska to Southern California

ZONE: lower intertidal, shallow subtidal

HABITATS: rocky shores, exposed and protected coasts

LENGTH: 0.4 in (1 cm)

COLOR: variable brown, gray, reddish, purple

SIMILAR SPECIES: Tucked Lirularia (p. 70)

Tucked Lirularia
LIRULARIA SUCCINCTA

A bit of detective work is required to find these miniature topsnails. Either hidden away in the gravel among rocks, or adhered to the underside of rocks, this mollusk only grows to a length or height of 0.25 inches (0.6 cm). Despite being easily glanced over and ignored, these snails are common along intertidal rocky shores and the shallow subtidal waters.

OTHER NAMES: Tucked Topsnail; *Margarites succinctus*

RANGE: Alaska to Southern California

ZONE: intertidal, shallow subtidal

HABITATS: rocky shores

LENGTH: to 0.25 in (0.6 cm)

COLOR: brown, purple, gray

SIMILAR SPECIES: Dall's Dwarf Turban (p. 69)

The snail comes in shades of brown, purple and gray, with a smooth surface texture because the ridges have a very low profile. The short spire is made up from four whorls, and there are some instances when the shell is flecked with white or dark patches. The Tucked Lirularia can be confused with Dall's Dwarf Turban because they are similar in size and color. However, the latter has a thick shell and distinct ridges running around the whorls. In British Columbia and Washington, the Pearly Topsnail (*L. lirulata*) looks similar to the Tucked Lirularia but has a proportionally higher spire, though it only grows to the same height as the Tucked Lirularia.

Checkered Periwinkle

LITTORINA SCUTULATA

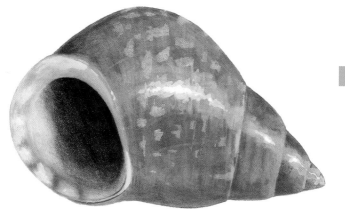

Periwinkles of many kinds litter the shores of the West Coast, and the Checkered is a likely find. They tolerate the high intertidal zone, and when the tide retreats they can be found tucked into crevices and among algal holdfasts or mussel beds. For a creature that spends so much time exposed to the air, a tight-fitting operculum (door) is very important, shutting the snail away inside its shell so no moisture is lost. It drifts about the rocks grazing on microscopic or larger alga (including the Sea Lettuce, p. 171), and suffers from the hungry attentions of starfish, especially the Six-rayed Sea Star (p. 109).

RANGE: Alaska to Southern California

ZONE: upper to lower intertidal

HABITATS: rocky shores

HEIGHT: to 0.5 in (1.3 cm)

COLOR: dark brown-black, white checkers

SIMILAR SPECIES: Sitka Periwinkle (p. 72)

This small periwinkle has a darkly colored shell that is frequently flecked with pale markings, giving a checkered effect. The surface of the shell, unless eroded, is smooth and slightly glossy. The variable Sitka Periwinkle occurs with it as does the similar Eroded Periwinkle (L. keenae), which generally has more markings and lighter colors. The Eroded Periwinkle is so tolerant that it can be found even higher up than the Checkered Periwinkle where the surf seldom sprays.

Sitka Periwinkle
LITTORINA SITKANA

From Washington northwards, the Sitka Periwinkle is found with its cousin, the Checkered Periwinkle. This periwinkle prefers rocky shores in quieter waters, but it can also be found on the open coast. Larger and sometimes prettier than the Checkered, this periwinkle has highly variable colors and sculpturing on its rounded shell.

From a dull gray to white banded caramel, it can be rather nondescript or have a delicate beauty. Look for it among the rocks and seaweeds in the high intertidal zone to lower levels.

RANGE: Alaska to Washington

ZONE: upper to middle intertidal

HABITATS: rocky shores

HEIGHT: to 0.8 in (2 cm)

COLOR: variable brown, gray, tan, pale bands

SIMILAR SPECIES: Checkered Periwinkle (p. 71)

This snail is absent from the subtidal waters because, if submerged for too long, it can suffocate. Thus it is confined to the higher intertidal regions, but must avoid full sunshine or risk frying up in the heat. It's a fine balance for the Sitka Periwinkle. Some shells might resemble the Checkered Periwinkle in color, but Sitka grows to a larger size, it lacks any checkered markings, and its spire is shorter.

Purple Dwarf Olive

OLIVELLA BIPLICATA

A celebrated find among beachcombers, these are highly polished shells with variable and beautiful colors. The Purple Dwarf Olive is elongated and tapered at both ends, rather resembling the slippery olive fruits. The pointed ends and smooth surface help the snail burrow through the sand, while the large foot propels it along. By day they are concealed well below the surface, perhaps just a slight dimple in the sand hinting at their presence. At night they are at the surface, the top of the shell often poking through.

RANGE: Alaska to Southern California

ZONE: middle to lower intertidal, subtidal to 150 ft (46 m)

HABITATS: sandy beaches

LENGTH: to 1.25 in (3.2 cm)

COLOR: variable purple, brown, gray

Gray and purple are the dominant colors, with brown stripes marking the suture of the short spire. The aperture is long, allowing the extensive foot to come out. A long siphon is used to suck water down from the surface. Purple Dwarf Olives gather in groups, perhaps as foraging parties, which certainly makes finding a mate easier in the vast expanses of sand. They sift the sand for decaying bits and pieces of organic material and occasionally take small prey, and are in turn victims of the other common sand-resident, Lewis's Moonsnail (p. 74).

Lewis's Moonsnail
POLINICES LEWISII

One of our largest intertidal snails, the almost round Lewis's Moonsnail can be found on sandy flats. From the large aperture a most enormous foot emerges, and is seemingly too much to squeeze back into the shell. The beige foot almost covers the shell, and to tuck it all away, water must be squeezed out through tiny pores. The large horny operculum (door) then seals it all in. The Moonsnail quickly suffocates when shut in, and would rather not do so for long.

RANGE: Alaska to Southern California

ZONE: lower intertidal, subtidal to 500 ft (152 m)

HABITATS: sandy flats, quiet waters

HEIGHT: to 5.5 in (14 cm)

COLOR: tan, brown

Burrowing through the sand, the Moonsnail particularly enjoys helpless clams stuck and buried where they thought they were protected. It wraps its foot around them and drills a hole with its radula. Once the contents are chewed out, the empty valves wash ashore with the distinctive hole, as shown on the Common Pacific Littleneck (p. 85). In turn, the Moonsnail is pursued by the Sunflower Star (p. 112) or occasionally its own kind. The mystical sand collars of this snail are formed around the shell when mucus is secreted with eggs inside. Sand quickly adheres to form a layered sandwich, 6 inches (15 cm) across, that washes ashore in summer.

Pacific Pink Scallop

CHLAMYS HASTATA HERICIA

Pretty in pink, this shell's beauty is often masked by an encrusting growth of camouflaging sponges. The upper valve, the more beautiful of the two, is illustrated—the paler, lower valve is pressed against the bottom. The rounded shells have a wavy margin, and darker growth rings in shades of pink and purple clearly show. Thin ribs are mixed with the more robust, and minute spines give a rough texture. The Smooth Pectin (*C. rubida*) looks the same but lacks these spines.

The arrival of a starfish is enough to send the Pink Scallop into a flapping frenzy, during which water is squished out of the shell to give some jet propulsion. When the scallop is living and agape, the water is being filtered for plankton, and a row of bright green eyes can be seen peeking out. More often you will come across this tasty morsel dead and on your plate, because it is a regular part of the commercial harvest. If you have been gathering them yourself, you would be wise to check with authorities about the levels of pollution in the area.

OTHER NAMES: Spiny Pink Scallop; Swimming Scallop

RANGE: Alaska to Southern California

ZONE: low-tide line and subtidal to 500 ft (152 m)

HABITATS: rocky reefs, sandy beds, quieter waters

LENGTH: 3.25 in (8.3 cm)

COLOR: white, yellow, pink, purple

SIMILAR SPECIES: Giant Rock Scallop (p. 76)

Giant Rock Scallop
CRASSODOMA GIGANTEA

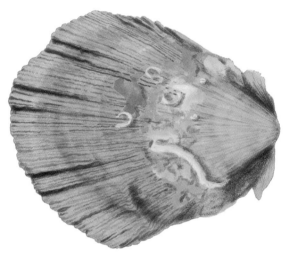

So tasty is this prized delicacy that it's the lucky naturalist who finds one intertidally. It is slow growing and lives up to 50 years, so remember the life you are removing if you want to harvest one. It can take up to 25 years to become full-grown, and quite a size it reaches, too. As a juvenile this scallop is free-swimming, and can be confused with the Pacific Pink Scallop. Pretty soon though, the scallop settles on a rock and sticks to it. Thereafter, the upper valve grows irregularly with the rock, and becomes encrusted with sponges, worms and anything else that thinks the scallop is a rock.

If observed alive, the flesh on a gaping shell is a brilliant orange, and small blue eyes are lined along the gap. Empty upper shells frequently turn up on the shore in fragments, but are easily identified by a deep purple stain in the hinge area. Aboriginal peoples once used the shells for jewelry and ground up the burnt shells to make paints. No doubt they didn't let the colorful flesh go to waste either.

OTHER NAMES: Purple-hinged Rock Scallop; *Hinnites giganteus*

RANGE: Alaska to California

ZONE: lower intertidal, subtidal to 150 ft (46 m)

HABITATS: rocky shores

LENGTH: to 10 in (25 cm)

COLOR: orange juvenile, encrusted adult

SIMILAR SPECIES: Pacific Pink Scallop (p. 75)

Pacific Shipworm
BANKIA SETACEA

Feared by the wooden shipbuilders of the past, the Pacific Shipworm can destroy wooden structures with its burrowing antics. Not a worm at all, but a greatly extended bivalve, the shipworm has two sharply serrated shells that it twists to carve a home in the wood. These tiny shells are white, and the burrows are lined with a calcareous secretion. At the rear end are two odd feathery structures called pallets. These tiered ornaments protect the two siphons that pump water in and out of the burrow, and serve as plugs for the entrance.

OTHER NAME: Feathery Shipworm

RANGE: Alaska to Southern California

ZONE: intertidal and subtidal

HABITATS: wood only

LENGTH: shell 0.25 in (0.6 cm), body to 3.3 ft (1 m)

COLOR: white shell

Young shipworms are free-swimming, soon settling on wood and burrowing into it. It is easier to follow the grain of the wood, and although a plank may be riddled with burrows, they never cross over each other. Digesting some of the wood, shipworms rely more on filtering the seawater through the burrow entrance, and extracting the planktonic wildlife. If you find some driftwood, try breaking it open to expose the mollusks within. If they have long since died, their shells and pallets might still be inside.

Baltic Macoma
MACOMA BALTHICA

A common find on beaches, this delicate little clam is often tinted in pretty shades of pink, blue, yellow or orange. The two valves are oval in shape, and still have the tattered remnants of a brown periostracum covering the outer edge of the shell. This tough coating has worn away from the umbones, the point near the shell's hinge, which represent the juvenile stages of the shell. See if you can detect the concentric growth lines from the umbo outwards, much like a tree's growth rings.

When alive, this bivalve has very long siphons that allow the mollusk to live up to 12 inches (30 cm) beneath the surface of muddy and sandy quiet areas. At low tide, the white siphons can sometimes be seen protruding in quiet tidepools. Luckily for the Baltic Macoma it never quite grows large enough to make it worthwhile eating for humans, but it does make for popular dining among certain ducks. The larger Bent-nosed Macoma is similar but has a distinctive curve to the shell and is not so round.

OTHER NAME: *M. inconspicua*

RANGE: Alaska to Northern California

ZONE: intertidal and subtidal to 130 ft (40 m)

HABITATS: quiet bays near open coast, estuaries

LENGTH: to 1.5 in (3.8 cm)

COLOR: white, with pale pink, blue, yellow or orange tint

SIMILAR SPECIES: Bent-nosed Macoma (p. 79)

Bent-nosed Macoma

MACOMA NASUTA

The thin white shells of the Bent-nosed Macoma have the unique habit of bending to one side. This habit is explained by the bivalve's preference for lying on its side and sending its siphons to the surface. Buried just 4 to 6 inches (10–15 cm) under the surface, the orange siphons extend upwards to sift for tasty sediments on the muddy sands. Once the clam has vacuumed up every morsel, it digs its way along to new territory, and starts again.

The Bent-nosed Macoma is common in bays and quieter waters along the open coast. Being only a few inches below the surface, it often falls victim to the dreaded Lewis's Moonsnail (p. 74). Clams that have fallen victim to this snail bear the distinctive drilled hole near the hinge, or umbo, of the valve. These dead shells fre-

OTHER NAME: Bent-nosed Clam

RANGE: Alaska to Northern California

ZONE: intertidal and subtidal to 150 ft (46 m)

HABITATS: muddy sands of bays, open coast

LENGTH: to 3 in (7.6 cm)

COLOR: mostly white

SIMILAR SPECIES: Baltic Macoma (p. 78), White Sand Macoma (p. 80)

quently wash up on the shore. Empty shells are plain white inside, much the same as the worn exterior. The Pointed Macoma (*M. inquinata*) is about same size but is not bent to one side.

White Sand Macoma

MACOMA SECTA

Empty shells are commonly found on the surface, while the living bivalve is buried deep beneath the sand, as much as 18 inches (46 cm) under the surface. Despite being so far under, the long white siphons still reach the surface. One siphon expels water while the other sucks it in along with bits of debris vacuumed up from the seafloor. Living at such depths offers the clam the best protection.

OTHER NAME: Sand Clam

RANGE: Alaska to Southern California

ZONE: intertidal and subtidal to 165 ft (50 m)

HABITATS: sand, quiet waters

LENGTH: to 4.5 in (11 cm)

COLOR: white

SIMILAR SPECIES: Bent-nosed Macoma (p. 79)

The shell is white, with a thin periostracum that adds hints of yellow and brown. Smoothly textured, the left valve is flatter than the right, and there is no bending as with the Bent-nosed Macoma with which it might be confused. The interior is also white. Considered to be fine dining, the White Sand Macoma seeks its revenge in having a gut full of sand, so be warned if you have not given the clam time to rinse out in clean seawater. Tiny pea crabs (*Pinnixa* sp.) often take up residence inside the clam where they have a safe home and a continual supply of food brought right to them—an easy life!

Geoduck

PANOPEA ABRUPTA

I f you lack determination and strength to dig deep, this is not the clam for you. The Geoduck, pronounced 'gooey-duck,' lies buried 3 to 5 feet (0.9–1.5 m) in the sand. And don't try to tug on the siphon to pull it out—it will just tear right off, and the animal will die. Weighing as much as 12 pounds (5.4 kg), and with a pale oblong shell measuring up to 8 inches (20 cm), this certainly is the King of the Clams.

The fused siphons are exceptionally long, so long that when a threatened clam tries to retract them, it can no longer squeeze all that flesh into its valves. When peaking just above the surface, the siphons are a giveaway for commercial divers, who then blow the sand clear with hydraulic equipment. Thus ends the life of a robust clam that can live to almost 150 years! Living so long, they are threatened by harvesting, so regulations for size are enforced. At six to seven years, the clam is of a harvestable size, and is said to be the finest clam on which to dine.

OTHER NAMES:	King Clam; *Panope generosa*
RANGE:	Alaska to California
ZONE:	lower intertidal, subtidal to 330 ft (101 m)
HABITATS:	muddy sand, bays
LENGTH:	to 8 in (20 cm)
COLOR:	gray or white shell
SIMILAR SPECIES:	Fat Gaper (p. 83)

Smooth Washington Clam
SAXIDOMUS GIGANTEUS

A nondescript white to gray shell, this abundant clam is the mainstay of the clam industry. The large oval shell is occasionally flecked with darker markings that are stains from iron sulfides. These compounds occur in the low-oxygen environment of the sandy gravel beds in which this clam likes to live. Growth rings on the shell show up as darker ridges and grooves. When growing slowly, in winter, the ridges are thick. The interior of the valves is a smooth white. When younger, the shell can be yellowish.

OTHER NAME: Butter Clam

RANGE: Alaska to Northern California

ZONE: middle to lower intertidal, subtidal at 130 ft (40 m)

HABITATS: sandy gravel shores

LENGTH: to 5.25 in (13.3 cm)

COLOR: pale yellow to gray-white

This clam is the base for the popular clam chowder, and has been an important part of the aboriginal diet for centuries. Despite reproducing quickly, regulations had to be set to prevent smaller clams from being harvested—which allows the populations to sustain themselves. Be sure to remove the black tips to the siphons, because nasty toxins are deposited there. The minimum harvestable size is 2.5 inches (6.4 cm). Clams that avoid capture can live for an impressive 20 years or more, and often have tiny pea crabs (*Pinnixa* sp.) living inside their shells.

Fat Gaper
TRESUS CAPAX

Fat and gaping, this clam can weigh as much as 4 pounds (1.8 kg), and the lengthy siphons are so voluminous that it cannot withdraw them into the two valves. If you are plodding about on mudflats, the clam retracts its fused siphons and shoots a jet of water into the air. Jump up and down, and you can really get them going! Tucked as much as 20 inches (51 cm) under the surface is a large bivalve, mostly chalky white, but with a brown edge where some of the periostracum remains. The siphon is dark brown, too.

Most Fat Gapers will be harboring a pair of tiny pea crabs (*Pinnixa* sp.) of various species. These grow to 1 inch (2.5 cm). The female pea crab grows so soft in the security of the bivalve that it would be a danger for her to wander about in her vulnerable shell. Males remain smaller and harder, and are thought to move from clam to clam. The flesh of commercially harvested Fat Gapers is not so wonderful, and is best minced up for chowders. The similar, fleshy Geoduck has a more oblong shell.

OTHER NAMES: Gaper Clam; Horse Clam

RANGE: British Columbia to Oregon

ZONE: intertidal and subtidal to 100 ft (30 m)

HABITATS: muddy sand, quiet bays

LENGTH: to 8 in (20 cm)

COLOR: white and brown

SIMILAR SPECIES: Geoduck (p. 81)

Nuttall's Cockle
CLINOCARDIUM NUTTALLI

This is a delightful shell to find, and if both valves are still joined at the hinge, when viewed from the ends they make a beautiful heart-shape. Strongly ribbed, the grayish shell is covered in a rich yellow to brown periostracum. The interior of the almost circular valves is a pale yellow-white. Well-defined ribs give a scalloped margin to the shell, and darker growth rings are evident. Much older Nuttall's Cockles have ribs that are worn down with age. Younger cockles may show some darker mottling on the shell.

OTHER NAMES: Basket Cockle; Heart Cockle

RANGE: Alaska to Southern California

ZONE: low intertidal, subtidal to 180 ft (55 m)

HABITATS: mud, sand, gravel, quiet waters

LENGTH: to 5.5 in (14 cm)

COLOR: gray, yellow-brown

The short siphons restrict the cockle from burrowing too deeply, and it often sits on or near the surface of muddy sands. To cope with this high-risk environment, the cockle has a muscular foot. When a hungry Sunflower Star (p. 112) gets too close, the cockle can flip and jump about, evading the grasping arms. Such strategies allow the cockle to live for up to 16 years. But, it is less adept at escaping commercial fishing—this cockle is a favorite for many.

Common Pacific Littleneck

PROTOTHACA STAMINEA

A poor digger, this Littleneck can be found in abundance in the firm, muddy gravel of quieter waters. It has short siphons, for which it gets the Littleneck name, that confine it close to the surface, making harvesting easy for enthusiasts hungry for some cockle flesh. Small jets of seawater mark their location, and if you are set on eating them, show some respect for the other organisms in the muddy gravel by using a small tool to extract your target. Minimum size harvestable is 1.5 inches (3.8 cm).

This bivalve has a finely textured surface from the many radiating and concentric ridges formed by the ribs and growth lines. Usually whitish in color, there can be tints of yellow, and darker brown markings often take the form of zigzags. The shell is quite thick, but not thick enough to deter the predatory Lewis's Moonsnail (p. 74) from drilling a hole through the shell near the hinge, and consuming the Littleneck. Victims of the Moonsnail wash up on the shore, so be sure to look for the telltale hole. The interior of the empty valves is white.

OTHER NAMES: Native Littleneck; Rock Cockle; Steamer Clam

RANGE: Alaska to Southern California

ZONE: middle to lower intertidal, shallow subtidal

HABITATS: coarse sand, mud, gravel, quieter waters

LENGTH: to 3 in (7.6 cm)

COLOR: tinted white, brown markings

SIMILAR SPECIES: Japanese Littleneck (p. 86)

Japanese Littleneck
TAPES JAPONICA

This accidental introduction from Japan has been given so many different names that it must surely be suffering from an identity crisis. Smoothly textured and elegantly long compared to the Common Pacific Littleneck, this bivalve found a corner of the coast where few other bivalves are found—high in the intertidal zone. Now it has become quite common, and supports a large industry in British Columbia and Washington, ousting the native littleneck. Short siphons restrict it to the top 4 inches (10 cm) of mud, sand or gravel, and they can easily be raked out.

OTHER NAMES: Manila Clam; Steamer Clam; *Venerupis philippinarum*

RANGE: British Columbia to Northern California

ZONE: upper intertidal

HABITATS: muddy sand, gravel

LENGTH: to 3 in (7.6 cm)

COLOR: gray, brown, streaked

SIMILAR SPECIES: Common Pacific Littleneck (p. 85)

With a base color of gray or brown, some Japanese Littlenecks are delicately marked with darker brown streaks or zigzags. The rear edge may be tinted in purple, and the smooth interior is mostly white tinted with yellow or purple. Favoring the mid- to high intertidal zone and not being buried very deep has its advantages and disadvantages—seldom does the bivalve fall prey to the Lewis's Moonsnail (p. 74), but huge numbers can be killed by cold winters.

Pacific Razor Clam
SILIQUA PATULA

This is a true prize for beachcombers. Buried just below the surface, its presence can be noted by a small dimple in the surface of the sand. Only the experienced hunter will be able to catch this swift bivalve. An uncovered razor clam can burrow out of sight in 10 seconds! These clams make for fine dining if you can catch them, but bear in mind that they are also food for the flatfish and starry flounder that forage for them when the tide is in. Luckily for the younger clams, they are protected from hungry human hunters, minimum size allowed being 4.5 inches (11 cm).

OTHER NAME: Northern Razor Clam

RANGE: Alaska to Northern California

ZONE: low-tide line, subtidal

HABITATS: sand, exposed beaches

LENGTH: 7 in (18 cm)

COLOR: caramel, olive, cream

The long thin shell is nicely polished and somewhat flattened. The periostracum, a tough outer coating on the shell, begins to wear away when it is pounded by surf or scorched by the sun. As it peels off, it reveals a whitish shell beneath. The caramel or olive-green colors on the shell show up the growth rings quite clearly. On the inside the shells are pale, with a hint of pink or purple.

Native Pacific Oyster
OSTREA LURIDA

Outshone by the much larger Giant Pacific Oyster, many consider the Native Pacific Oyster to have a superior taste. Only growing to 3.5 inches (8.9 cm), its much smaller size may also be a deterrent because many more oysters must be collected for the same quantity of meat. Once abundant along much of the coast, this oyster has shown sensitivity to pollutants, especially pulp mill effluent, and attempts are being made to reintroduce it back into Oregon estuaries.

OTHER NAME: Olympia Oyster

RANGE: Alaska to Southern California

ZONE: low-tide line, subtidal to 165 ft (50 m)

HABITATS: flats, tidepools, estuaries, firm substrates

LENGTH: to 3.5 in (8.9 cm)

COLOR: cream and gray, heavily marked

SIMILAR SPECIES: Giant Pacific Oyster (p. 89)

This oyster is found in many intertidal habitats such as mudflats, gravel banks, tidepools, estuaries, rocks, pilings and other shells. The valves grow rather irregularly, shaped by the substrate onto which they are attached, and no two shells will look the same. Some are rather round while others become more elongated. The exterior is cream to grayish with white or darker markings, and there are visible but irregular growth rings. The interior is a smooth white with green or blue tints. These oysters are rather indecisive about what sex to be and will switch from being female one year to male in the next.

Giant Pacific Oyster

CRASSOTREA GIGAS

This giant of an oyster was introduced early in the 20th century and has become so successful that huge banks of them can be seen in the intertidal zone of protected beaches and estuaries. It is much hardier than the diminutive Native Pacific Oyster. It grows to 12 inches (30 cm) in length, and its lower valve is attached to other oyster shells or rocky substrates. The shell is gray to white, with a clean white interior. The shell is covered with wavy flutings and molds its shape to the object it has decided to grow on.

OTHER NAME: Japanese Oyster

RANGE: Alaska to Northern California

ZONE: intertidal and subtidal to 20 ft (6.1 m)

HABITATS: firm surfaces, other oysters, estuaries, quiet waters

LENGTH: to 12 in (30 cm)

COLOR: cream and gray

SIMILAR SPECIES: Native Pacific Oyster (p. 88)

Once scattered in population, this oyster has now become the greatest contributor to the oyster industry, with harvesting of individuals that are 5 to 6 inches (13–15 cm) in length. The oyster is not only a victim of our enormous appetites. The West Coast has become a battleground of introduced species, with the Atlantic Oyster Drill (*Urosalpinx cinerea*) relishing these juicy bivalves from the western Pacific. It also has to endure the attentions of starfish. There is not much the oysters can do about either, because they are firmly adhered to their place.

California Mussel
MYTILUS CALIFORNIENSIS

Large and unmistakable, this mussel thrives in the pounding surf of open coasts. Strong, protein-rich byssal threads extend from the foot of the mussel and cling tenaciously to the rock or to other mussels. Huge 'beds' frequently form in bands along the rocky shores. One atop another, the unfortunate individuals at the bottom may have a hard time holding onto the rock, and large waves can tear out chunks of the bed. This exposes the rock once again, and new colonies will form.

RANGE: Alaska to Southern California

ZONE: middle to lower intertidal, subtidal to 330 ft (101 m)

HABITATS: rocks, pilings, exposed coasts

LENGTH: to 8 in (20 cm), larger subtidally

COLOR: blue-black, brown

SIMILAR SPECIES: Blue Mussel (p. 91)

The thick beautiful shells are usually blue, with hints of brown. The tough periostracum that produces these colors can be seen peeling off the surface of dead shells. Low-profile ribs radiate out from the hinge of the shells. The interior is a glossy blue and white, and a few small but worthless pearls may be found. If mussels are a favorite for you, be warned that summer harvesting can be dangerous because the orange flesh accumulates the paralytic poisons from the notorious 'red tide.'

Blue Mussel
MYTILUS EDULIS

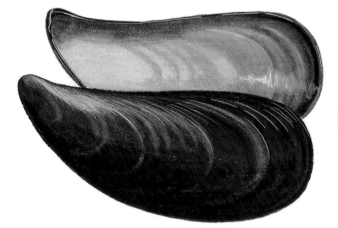

Smaller than the California Mussel and less hardy, these delicate mussels are found in protected waters and often where there is low salinity (when fresh water mixes with seawater). Where conditions are right, the Blue Mussel can be seen growing along with the robust California Mussel. The Blue Mussel can form dense mats in abundance. These beds make excellent habitats for many other organisms that enjoy the shelter and protection between the shells. While brown shells are quite common, most of the long elegant shells are blue-black. Blue Mussels lack the ribs and uneven texture of the California Mussel. The interior of the valves is blue-white.

Attached to rocks and wood, especially pilings, these thin-shelled bivalves are a favorite food source for crabs, birds and starfish. Their small size deters many a human hunter, and they avoid the predatory whelks of the open coast by living in quiet waters. As the gentle waves fall over them, the mussels take water into their shells where they filter it for tiny particles of food.

OTHER NAMES: Edible Mussel; Bay Mussel; *M. trossulus*

RANGE: Alaska to Southern California

ZONE: middle to lower intertidal, subtidal to 16 ft (4.9 m)

HABITATS: quiet waters, rock, wood

LENGTH: to 4 in (10 cm)

COLOR: blue-black, brown

SIMILAR SPECIES: California Mussel (p. 90)

Gumboot Chiton

CRYPTOCHITON STELLERI

The giant of all chitons, this one is so large that it becomes easy not to notice, looking like a nondescript growth on a rock. While other chitons show their distinctive plates on their back, this one has a girdle that completely covers it. Underneath are eight bony plates that sometimes wash ashore and have earned the name of 'butterfly shells' because of their shape.

OTHER NAME: Giant Pacific Chiton

RANGE: Alaska to Southern California

ZONE: lower intertidal, subtidal to 65 ft (20 m)

HABITATS: rocky beaches

LENGTH: to 13 in (33 cm)

COLOR: reddish-brown

Most Gumboots are reddish-brown with a rough texture, and they are stuck to the rock with a large muscular foot. Underneath, the foot is yellow. Gumboots are so large that they can be knocked off their footing by rough seas and may even turn up stranded on the beach. This chiton slowly creeps around grazing on encrusting and fleshy algae. Living for 20 years, this mass of flesh has surprisingly few predators, although the Lurid Rocksnail (p. 57) has been known to chew away at its surface, leaving little scars. Historically, it has been used as a food source by aboriginal peoples, but, unless you are fond of tough rubber, the Gumboot does not come recommended.

Black Katy Chiton
KATHARINA TUNICATA

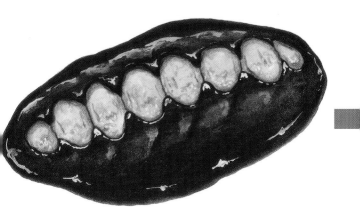

Of all the chitons, the Black Katy Chiton is the one you are most likely to see. Common on exposed coasts in the middle of the intertidal zone, this chiton is not sensitive to light, and will sit boldly atop exposed rocks. Other chitons tend to hide away. This primitive mollusk resembles a limpet with a large sucking foot that holds on so tightly to the rock. The Black Katy Chiton moves about slowly grazing on algae.

OTHER NAME: Leather Chiton
RANGE: Alaska to California
ZONE: middle intertidal
HABITATS: rocky shores
LENGTH: to 5 in (13 cm)
COLOR: pale plates, black girdle

The eight plates are visible on the back, but the shiny coal-black girdle covers most of each plate. The Black Katy Chiton adheres so well to rock it can be hard to remove. If you are determined to study this animal further, use the blunt side of a blade to gently lift the animal off—it is easily injured. But if you can resist the temptation, then the chiton is sure to be happier. On the underside, the foot is salmon-colored, and the mouth can be seen at one end. In response to being removed from its snug rock, the chiton will begin to curl up to protect its soft underside.

Merten's Chiton
LEPIDOZONA MERTENSII

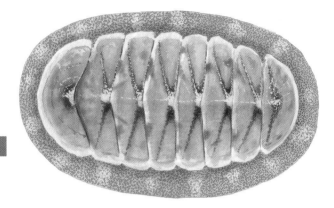

A little bit of searching is required to turn up these little ocean gems. Merten's Chiton is most often stuck to the underside of rocks in the intertidal zone, but also lives in deeper water. When turning rocks in the hunt for this mollusk, be sure to replace them very carefully so as not to damage the chiton and the wealth of other creatures living there.

RANGE: Alaska to Southern California

ZONE: intertidal, subtidal to 300 ft (91 m)

HABITATS: quiet waters, rock, wood

LENGTH: to 2 in (5 cm)

COLOR: variable browns, reds

SIMILAR SPECIES: Lined Chiton (p. 95)

This chiton is intricately marked. Unusually for intertidal chitons, the girdle surrounding the plates is made from tiny scales. The girdle is reddish-brown with paler patches that may appear as bands. The plates are very obvious and delicately marked in oranges, browns and reds and occasional white patches. Underneath, the foot runs for most of its length, and down either side of the foot are gills that allow this quiet creature to obtain oxygen from circulating water. This chiton is sometimes confused with Cooper's Chiton (*L. cooperi*), which is a dull brown version found in Washington and Oregon. Also, check that you are not looking at the Lined Chiton.

Lined Chiton
TONICELLA LINEATA

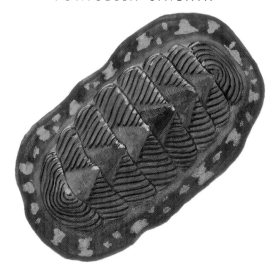

The Lined Chiton is the prize of the Pacific coast and a feast for the eyes. Fortunately for us they can be clearly and commonly visible on rocks exposed at low tide, although close attention is required to pick them out. The chiton is so heavily lined with many colors that it blends surprisingly well with its environment, often avoiding detection. When the surge channels are quiet, be sure to look along the walls, as well as near patches of pink encrusting algae. These jewels also turn up near the stunning Purple Sea Urchins (p. 117).

RANGE: Alaska to Southern California

ZONE: lower intertidal, subtidal to 180 ft (55 m)

HABITATS: rocky shores

LENGTH: to 2 in (5 cm)

COLOR: highly variable, mostly red

SIMILAR SPECIES: Merten's Chiton (p. 94)

The patterns are highly variable and may involve just about every color of the rainbow. Most come reddish, with a smooth girdle blotched in creamy colors. The eight plates running down the back are busily lined in purple, black, white, pink, red, yellow and many other colors, depending on the individual chiton and where it has chosen to live. They creep about the rocks consuming algae and anything growing on the algae, and are themselves the target of the Ochre Sea Star (p. 111).

Hairy Mopalia
MOPALIA CILIATA

This dark-colored chiton gets its name from the short hair-like growths found on the girdle surrounding the plates running down the back. These bony plates are exquisitely designed, and on close inspection have the texture of chain-mail. It is hard to work out which end is the head of this mollusk—look at the end plates and the one with thin radiating lines marks the front of the chiton. A small notch is occasionally present at the rear end. The plates down the back are articulated, allowing the chiton to flex and change its flattened shape so that it can fit snugly against uneven rocky surfaces.

RANGE: Alaska to Southern California

ZONE: middle to lower intertidal, subtidal to 16 ft (4.9 m)

HABITATS: rocky shores, crevices, mussel beds

LENGTH: to 3 in (7.6 cm)

COLOR: gray-green, sometimes mottled

SIMILAR SPECIES: Mossy Chiton (p. 97)

In shades of gray-green, sometimes mottled with light or dark patches, the Hairy Mopalia blends in well with its surroundings. It prefers the mid- to low intertidal zone of rocky beaches. By day it hides in rocky crevices or among mussel beds, but by night it becomes active, feeding on both plants and animals, from microscopic algae to sponges and bryozoans. On rather dull days, it may also start to move about.

Mossy Chiton
MOPALIA MUSCOSA

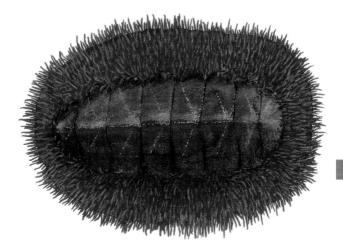

A thick brown girdle covered in bristly hairs gives this chiton a mossy texture and appearance. Mossy Chitons also come in gray-green hues. The dark plates, exposed down the middle of its back, will sometimes have a pale line down the middle. This line is often obscured by an overgrowth of organisms that have made the chiton's back their home. Tubeworms, algae and barnacles are just some of the many organisms that you might find hitching a ride.

This species is a common chiton found between the tides on rocky shores. Its ability to tolerate low salinity allows it to venture into estuaries as well. The Mossy Chiton makes a home on a favorite patch of rock. It never roams too far, and after a night of foraging and scraping away for food on the surface of rocks, it

RANGE: Alaska to Southern California
ZONE: upper to lower intertidal
HABITATS: rocky shores, tidepools, estuaries
LENGTH: to 3.5 in (8.9 cm)
COLOR: brown, gray-green
SIMILAR SPECIES: Hairy Mopalia (p. 96)

will return to its favorite spot. The Hairy Mopalia has shorter bristles, and the Woody Chiton (*M. lignosa*) comes in similar dark brown shades but many other colors as well. The conspicuous Ochre Sea Star (p. 111) makes a meal out of chitons.

Sea Mouse
AEOLIDIA PAPILLOSA

Shaggy like a bedraggled mouse, this nudibranch has so many cerata, or fleshy projections, on its back that it looks hairy. There is a cerata-free stripe down the middle of the back, and two sensory rhinophores (tentacles) rise out of the bare patch on the head and probably function much like a nose. Two additional fleshy tentacles protrude off the front, helping the sea slug guide its way along. Mostly pale in color and somewhat translucent, there is often a tint of pink, mauve or beige. The cerata are wide at the base and narrow to a point that is much paler in color, sometimes white.

The Sea Mouse is found in many habitats, especially rocky areas and among Eelgrass (p. 179). Its appearance allows it to blend in extremely well among colonies of anemones, especially the Aggregating Anemone (p. 121) on which it loves to dine. Some nudibranchs benefit from eating anemones because they can store the anemone's stinging cells at the end of their cerata, defending themselves with this stolen weaponry. Just how they get the nematocysts, or stinging cells, there intact and untriggered remains a mystery.

OTHER NAME: Shag-rug Nudibranch

RANGE: Alaska to Northern California

ZONE: intertidal, subtidal to 2950 ft (899 m)

HABITATS: rocky shores, Eelgrass beds

LENGTH: to 4 in (10 cm)

COLOR: variable pale shades

Sea Lemon
ANISODORIS NOBILIS

Lemon in color, this nudibranch does indeed look like a piece of abandoned fruit. Some come in stronger shades of orange, but all have scattered black spots between the tiny tubercles that give them a rough texture. The Sea Lemon is one of the largest sea slugs of the Pacific coast, growing to 4 inches (10 cm) intertidally and to as much as 8 inches (20 cm) subtidally. Look for them tucked away under fronds of seaweed on rocky shores.

At the head end are two rhinophores, and at the rear is a plume of frilly gills fringed in white. The Sea Lemon is a hermaphrodite, each one being both male and female—this must surely make finding a partner easy! When provoked, these harmless-looking nudibranchs emit a strong odor with fruity overtones, thought to dissuade any predator from consuming them. Sponges are the mainstays of the Sea Lemon's diet. Another sea lemon, the Monterey Doris (*Archidoris monteyerensis*), is commonly found intertidally, but it does not grow so large and has black markings scattered between and up the tiny tubercles on the sea slug's back.

RANGE: Southern British Columbia to California

ZONE: intertidal, subtidal to 750 ft (229 m)

HABITATS: rocky shores, under seaweed

LENGTH: to 8 in (20 cm)

COLOR: yellow, orange, dark spots

Yellow-edged Cadlina

CADLINA LUTEOMARGINATA

This whitish nudibranch is delicately fringed in bright yellow, and each tubercle on its back is tinged in yellow. Look under rocks and in tidepools near the low-tide line. The pale form of the Nanaimo Nudibranch (*Acanthodoris nanaimoensis;* which also comes in a dark phase) can be confused with the Yellow-edged Cadlina, but usually comes with tints of maroon on the gills at the rear and on the rhinophores. The plume of gills is used to extract oxygen from the water, much like a fish's gills.

RANGE: Alaska to Southern California

ZONE: lower intertidal, subtidal to 75 ft (23 m)

HABITATS: rocky shores, under rocks, tidepools

LENGTH: to 3 in (7.6 cm)

COLOR: whitish, yellow markings

When gently touched, the surface of the sea slug feels very rough. This texture is created by tiny spicules that are derived from sponges, which use it in their skeletal matrix. The nudibranch eats the sponge and puts the spicules to good use, instead of excreting them. A spiky meal is much less appetizing to potential predators. Few creatures relish eating nudibranchs because they can smell bad, taste bad, feel too spiky, or are even armed with stinging cells. So, for the most part, nudibranchs can go about their business of eating uninterrupted.

Ring-spotted Doris

DISCODORIS SANDIEGENSIS

This appealing nudibranch comes boldly marked with dark leopard-like spots and rings set against a creamy base color. It is commonly found throughout the region on the sides of boulders, under ledges and where seaweed can offer some protection. In the north of its range, the Ring-spotted Doris tends to have more rings, while in the south the rings can be so few in number that they seem completely lacking. Other Ring-spotted Dorises are dark instead of cream, especially in shades of chocolate-brown.

As with many nudibranchs, sponges are a favored food item, especially the encrusting Purple Sponge (p. 153). A rasping radula inside the mouth on the underside of the slug is used to bite away at the sponge. Tiny hairy projections on the skin give a rough feeling to this mollusk, and the tuft of gills at the rear can be retracted inside. Each Ring-spotted Doris is both male and female, and after mating with another individual, the sea slug lays a curly ribbon of white eggs in protected nooks.

OTHER NAMES: Ringed Nudibranch; Leopard Nudibranch; *Diaulula sandiegensis*

RANGE: Alaska to Southern California

ZONE: lower intertidal, subtidal to 110 ft (34 m)

HABITATS: rocky shores, crevices, seaweed

LENGTH: to 3.5 in (8.9 cm)

COLOR: cream to brown, dark spots

Opalescent Nudibranch
HERMISSENDA CRASSICORNIS

This flamboyant sea slug graces the entire Pacific coast, and it is one of the commonest nudibranchs to be found. A slender, elegant body has many hair-like projections (cerata) in bands down each side of the body. The foot is translucent and lined with white or blue. The cerata are beautifully and variably presented with white, orange and brown markings—the brown is an extension of digestive glands from the gut. Most distinctive is the vivid orange line down the middle of the back, while the rest of the colors and markings can be quite variable.

OTHER NAMES: Hermissenda; *Phidiana crassicornis*

RANGE: British Columbia to California

ZONE: lower intertidal, subtidal to 110 ft (34 m)

HABITATS: rocky shores, tidepools, Eelgrass beds

LENGTH: to 3 in (7.6 cm)

COLOR: variable, pale with orange markings

Tidepools on rocky shores, mudflats and beds of Eelgrass (p. 179) that are near the low-tide line are all the haunts of this aggressive carnivore. These nudibranchs readily consume small anemones, bryozoans, sea squirts, worms and much more. They are even fond of taking a bite out of each other, perhaps in defense of a favorite feeding territory. When they consume prey with stinging cells, such as sea anemones, they store up the stinging cells in the ends of their cerata to aid in their own defense.

Rough-mantled Doris

ONCHIDORIS BILAMELLATA

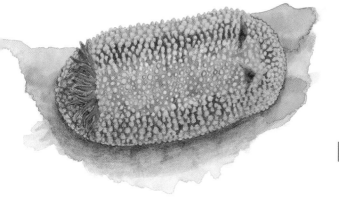

Mottled in creams and browns, a keen eye is needed to detect this small nudibranch that barely reaches 1 inch (2.5 cm) in length. It is found along most of the Pacific coast from well above the low-tide line to the shallow subtidal waters. Rocks and pilings are favorite locations for this sea slug, especially where its favorite food is found. When young, they dine on bryozoans, but as they age and get larger, they shift to consuming Acorn Barnacles (p. 135).

The Rough-mantled Doris gets its name from its heavily textured back. It is covered with knobby projections that are larger on the sides than in the middle of the back. These club-shaped tubercles are mostly translucent, and inside they are reinforced with spicules that make the sea slug spiky and less appetizing. Towards the rear end is a densely packed mass of gills that are used to obtain oxygen from the seawater. The sea slugs, much like their land equivalents, are mollusks that have lost their shells, and have instead developed many other means of protection.

RANGE: Alaska to Southern California

ZONE: intertidal, subtidal to 25 ft (7.6 m)

HABITATS: rocky shores, pilings

LENGTH: to 1 in (2.5 cm)

COLOR: variable cream, brown, mottled

Sea Clown Nudibranch

TRIOPHA CATALINAE

Dazzling and comical, the Sea Clown Nudibranch can be seen in the tidepools of rocky shores. So bright and cheerful, they are hard to miss. The whitish body is covered in stubby protuberances, each of which is tipped in strong orange. The sensory rhinophores (tentacles) and the frilled ring of gills are also colorfully tipped. The head is broad and bears several branched and forward-pointing projections.

These sea slugs are most often about 1 inch (2.5 cm) in length, but can grow to an impressive 6 inches (15 cm). Unlike many other nudibranchs with their tough and hardened skins, these ones are rather squishy and flimsy, and one would imagine that they would make delectable eating. However, these noticeable slugs are never touched, happily cruising about the tidepool unharmed—the brilliant orange may serve as a deterrent and warning that they don't taste good. Many nudibranchs, in calm pools, have the talent of walking upside-down along the undersurface of the water. This ability saves having to deal with all the obstacles of a trip along the bottom. Touch them gently and they will rapidly sink.

RANGE: Alaska to Southern California

ZONE: intertidal, subtidal to 110 ft (34 m)

HABITATS: rocky shores, tidepools, kelp

LENGTH: to 6 in (15 cm)

COLOR: orange flecks on white

Stubby Squid

ROSSIA PACIFICA

The pretty Stubby Squid is one of the best reasons to go down to the tidepools at night with a flashlight. Sometimes found in large tidepools, but more usually in subtidal zones, this squid has beautiful swimming control. Water is propelled out of the mantle cavity, shooting the squid backwards, and a small fin around the edge of the mantle provides subtle control.

A cluster of grabbing tentacles, for seizing fish and shrimp, surrounds the beak-like mouth. This squid will often sit on the bottom with its arms over its head. To help it blend in further with its environment, the speckles on its skin can change color very quickly. This talent is shared by many squid, and it is remarkable to watch. Small pigment patches are contracted or expanded to change the color density. The Stubby Squid is shorter and, well, stubbier than the sleek, common Opalescent Squid (*Loligo opalescens*), the market squid, producer of 5-inch (13-cm) long egg-cases that wash ashore and resemble pale jelly sausages. Peek inside and you might make out the tiny squid embryos.

RANGE: Alaska to California
ZONE: lower intertidal, subtidal to 1200 ft (366 m)
HABITATS: tidepools, inshore waters
LENGTH: 5 in (13 cm)
COLOR: variable, often red

Giant Pacific Octopus
OCTOPUS DOFLEINI

Persistent searching of large tidepools at the low-tide line may reveal this fabulous mollusk. Advanced well beyond its snail relatives, these creatures are highly intelligent and, despite a fierce and dangerous reputation, have a shy disposition. Smaller individuals turn up in tidepools, and the real babies might be mistaken for the Red Octopus (*O. rubescens*), which only grows to about 6 inches (15 cm) and lacks the folded skin. Cold water is preferred, so intertidal sightings are rare south of Washington.

RANGE: Alaska to Washington

ZONE: lower intertidal, subtidal to 600 ft (180 m)

HABITATS: tidepools, crevices, caves

LENGTH: arm spread 20 ft (6.1 m)

COLOR: variable, often reddish-brown

At the base of the eight arms is a powerful beak-like mouth used to hack crabs, snails and a lot of other prey apart. Stalking and lunging are its preferred tactics for ambush, and seldom can the target escape the suction of the cups on the arm. If handled roughly, an octopus will let you know by striking with its sharp beak—so respect them! Like the Stubby Squid (p. 105), the octopus is gifted at changing its color to blend in with its home. A pile of empty shells and chunks of crabs reveals the den of an octopus.

Leather Star
DERMASTERIAS IMBRICATA

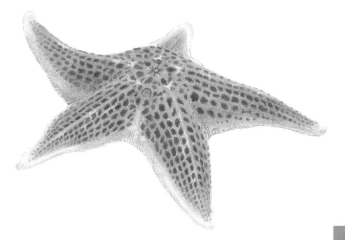

To some it smells of garlic, to others it has overtones of exploded gunpowder. Either way, the touch of the Leather Star is enough to make some species of anemone release their tenacious foothold on a rock and swim for safety. This starfish is a predator of anemones, urchins and cucumbers of the marine type. The mouth is in the middle of the underside, and rows of small tube feet on the underside of each arm help the animal move. Its name derives from the smooth and slippery skin on the upper surface, which gives it a leathery texture.

The Leather Star has five short arms and a robust build, but it is not as stocky as the variably colored Bat Star. The intricate patterns are usually made up of red or orange patches set against a blue-gray background. They are most often encountered in the low-intertidal zone among rocks and occasionally in sandy areas. Protected sounds and bays are preferred, and pilings or sea walls can be good places to hunt for them.

RANGE: Alaska to Southern California

ZONE: lower intertidal, subtidal to 300 ft (91 m)

HABITATS: rocks, sheltered bays, sounds, sea walls, pilings

WIDTH: to 8 in (20 cm)

COLOR: red on blue-gray

SIMILAR SPECIES: Bat Star (p. 110)

Troschel's Sea Star

EVASTERIAS TROSCHELII

This elegant sea star inhabits the rocks and soft-bottomed shores of the protected coasts. In the southerly parts of its range, it is increasingly rare, and it is seldom seen in Oregon. It is frequently confused with the Ochre Sea Star, despite some obvious differences between the two. Troschel's Sea Star has five rays that are more slender and a small central disk. It also comes in a whole range of colors from green to blue-gray, but most often in shades of red and orange.

RANGE: Alaska to Northern California

ZONE: lower intertidal, subtidal to 230 ft (70 m)

HABITATS: rocks, soft bottoms, protected waters, tidepools, mussel beds

WIDTH: to 22 in (56 cm)

COLOR: highly variable, red to blue-gray

SIMILAR SPECIES: Ochre Sea Star (p. 111)

Troschel's Sea Star often turns up with the Ochre Sea Star near the low-tide line, especially in mussel beds and tidepools. Closer inspection of its surface will reveal many tiny whitish spines that do not form any patterns as they do with the Ochre Sea Star. Its diet is composed mainly of mussels, barnacles and limpets. On the tip of each arm of a sea star is a small reddish eye that has only simple vision, and off to one side of the central disk is a small round plate through which water passes in and out.

Six-rayed Sea Star
LEPTASTERIAS HEXACTIS

This small sea star comes in shades of green to black, orange and tan, and is occasionally mottled, too. Rather inconspicuous because of its often drab colors, this sea star requires some effort to find—look under loose rocks and boulders on the protected and open coast. The Six-rayed Sea Star is distinct for having six rays, instead of the more normal five and a feathery-looking texture from closely packed spines.

This sea star gets its other common name, Brooding Star, from the female's unusual winter behavior. Standing on the tips of her rays, she carefully tends a mass of yellowish eggs in the cavity for over a month, until they hatch. She then guards the tiny young until she feels confident that the baby stars can cling to the rocks on their own. After nearly two months, she can finally start to look for food and eat again. This sea star eats mollusks—including the exquisite Lined Chiton (p. 95)—and barnacles, and scavenges on the occasional dead meat drifting its way.

OTHER NAME: Brooding Star

RANGE: British Columbia to Southern California

ZONE: lower intertidal, shallow subtidal

HABITATS: rocky shores, under rocks, tidepools, mussel beds

WIDTH: to 3.5 in (8.9 cm)

COLOR: highly variable, black to mottled tan

Bat Star
ASTERINA MINIATA

Wonderfully geometric with five stout arms, or rays, this sea star is locally abundant in parts of Vancouver Island and Northern California, but is seldom seen in between. Where it is common, its bright colors make it conspicuous against rocks and in tidepools. Once in a while the Bat Star will have more than five arms, sometimes as many as nine. It gets its name from the webbed arms, likened to a bat's wing. Commonest shades include bright reds and oranges, as well as darker shades of green, brown and even purple, with mottling in some.

OTHER NAMES: Sea Bat; *Patiria miniata*

RANGE: British Columbia to Southern California

ZONE: lower intertidal, subtidal to 950 ft (290 m)

HABITATS: rocks, tidepools, open coasts

WIDTH: to 8 in (20 cm)

COLOR: highly variable, red, green, brown, purple, mottled

SIMILAR SPECIES: Leather Star (p. 107)

A Bat Star is not a fussy eater, happy to dine on almost anything. This sea star extrudes its stomach out of its mouth and wraps it around the food of its choice, digesting externally before swallowing. Algae and kelp are frequently consumed, but small animals do just as well. On the Bat Star's underside, look for the small brown Bat Star Worm (*Ophiodromus pugettensis*) living in the grooves. The Leather Star is occasionally mistaken for the Bat Star—note that it has distinctive patterns, a smooth texture and slightly longer arms.

Ochre Sea Star

PISASTER OCHRACEUS

The striking orange form of this sea star is a common sight on exposed rocky shores. Clinging to wave-swept rocks, these rough-skinned sea stars are also dark brown or purple, and blunt white spines give a coarse texture to the skin. A clean appearance is maintained by tiny pincers that peck and pull apart anything that lands on them. The sight or smell of this sea star is enough to send many intertidal organisms running, crawling, slithering or jumping for their lives.

Mussel and barnacle beds are the Ochre Sea Star's favorite domain—the appetite and abundance of which determine the lower limit of mussel beds. With its tube feet, it gradually pulls the shells apart, inserts its stomach and slowly digests the contents—all of which can take a couple of days! These beauties are the sad victims of human ignorance. So hard and colorful are they that people take them home as beach souvenirs thinking they will dry up and look great on the mantle piece. Instead, they rot and smell terrible, so please leave them where they belong.

OTHER NAMES: Purple Sea Star; Pacific Sea Star

RANGE: Alaska to Southern California

ZONE: intertidal, subtidal to 300 ft (91 m)

HABITATS: exposed rocky shores

WIDTH: to 14 in (36 cm)

COLOR: orange-ochre, brown or purple

SIMILAR SPECIES: Troschel's Sea Star (p. 108)

Sunflower Star

PYCNOPODIA HELIANTHOIDES

The largest sea star in the world graces our western shores, and it is a spectacle worth looking for. This sea star is subtidal, venturing into intertidal waters to forage, and occasionally getting stranded in pools as the tide goes out. Some have been measured at up to a staggering 40 inches (102 cm) across, though most come smaller than this. When young they have six arms, but as they age new arms are added until there are more than 20.

These orange, brown or purplish sea stars are soft in appearance, gentle to the touch and brittle when handled—arms readily break off, so don't handle them, just watch! They are rapid movers, at least when compared to other sea stars, and the arrival of this giant in a tidepool is enough to send just about every organism nearby into a major panic, and the exodus begins. Purple Sea Urchins (p. 117) are a favored food especially, and their clean 'tests'—skeletons—can be plentiful, symbols of the ransack preceding your arrival. Just about every creature is eaten, including other species of sea stars.

RANGE: Alaska to Southern California

ZONE: lower intertidal, subtidal to 1450 ft (442 m)

HABITATS: rocky shores, soft bottoms

WIDTH: to 40 in (102 cm)

COLOR: variable orange, red, brown or purple

Daisy Brittle Star

OPHIOPHOLIS ACULEATA

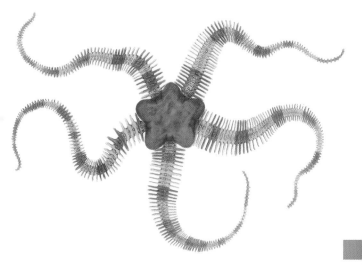

D aisy Brittle Stars are fascinating creatures that rapidly wriggle away in a sinuous writhing motion if disturbed from their hiding places. They can frequently be found tucked under rocks or in small crevices. Handle them carefully, and don't be surprised if a leg falls off—this brittleness is how they get their name. A lost leg will soon regrow, and just maybe the brittle star will thank you if you decide to spare it this inconvenience.

Daisy Brittle Stars come in an infinite combination of colors, but most common is the red and tan mix. The central disk is very prominent, more so than with related sea stars. It has a scalloped edge forming five lobes, and from each indent a spiny leg emerges. They are much more agile than sea stars, using their limbs instead of tiny tube feet to move about. Some arms will pull while others will push, but the general appearance is a wriggling mass of legs. A tiny cousin hidden under rocks is the Dwarf Brittle Star (*Axiognathus squamata*) that is gray and grows to just over 1 inch (2.5 cm).

> RANGE: Alaska to Southern California
>
> ZONE: lower intertidal, subtidal to over 5000 ft (1524 m)
>
> HABITATS: under rocks, crevices, algal holdfasts, tidepools
>
> WIDTH: to 3 in (7.6 cm)
>
> COLOR: highly variable, commonly red and tan

Eccentric Sand Dollar

DENDRASTER EXCENTRICUS

A popular souvenir of beachcombers, the flattened Sand Dollar is commonly found on sandy beaches. The familiar gray or white dollar represents the skeleton, or 'test,' of the urchin, which usually lives just below the low-tide line in sandy-bottomed areas. When living, the test is covered with tiny spines that give it a dark brown or purple color. Crowds of Sand Dollars can sometimes be seen vertically lodged in the sand filtering tiny particles from the water currents. Tiny hairs move the trapped particles towards the mouth.

OTHER NAME: Sand Cookie

RANGE: Alaska to Southern California

ZONE: low-tide line, subtidal to 130 ft (40 m)

HABITATS: sandy areas, sheltered bays

WIDTH: to 3.2 in (8 cm)

COLOR: gray-white test, dark spines

In rough weather or at low tide, the Sand Dollar uses movable spines to bury itself further into the sand and flatten down so as not to expose itself to strong currents. Despite this activity, some will still end up stranded on the shore after a heavy storm. Here, they die and the spines are gradually washed away, revealing the characteristic five-petaled flower etched on the test, and hinting at the Sand Dollar's ancestral connection to sea stars. This off-centre pattern marks where the tube feet once emerged.

Green Sea Urchin
STRONGYLOCENTROTUS DROEBACHIENSIS

In the protected sounds and tidepools of the open coast, this spiny creature can be so abundant that it is hard not to tread on it. Common to the north, this urchin is absent from the coasts of Oregon southwards. The Green Sea Urchin has short, pale green spines set against a green-brown 'test' (skeleton). The spines are densely packed. Movement is achieved very slowly, with a gentle, co-ordinated arrangement of spines allowing it to graze on new patches of algae. In the middle of the underside is the mouth, which is made up of five triangular tooth-like structures that chip away at the food.

RANGE: Alaska to Washington

ZONE: intertidal, subtidal to over 3500 ft (1067 m)

HABITATS: sandy areas, sheltered bays

WIDTH: to 4 in (10 cm)

COLOR: green, green-brown

SIMILAR SPECIES: juvenile Purple Sea Urchin (p. 117)

These urchins enjoy rocky shores as well as softer-bottomed areas, and they are the most numerous urchin in protected waters. They are found between the tides as well as subtidally to considerable depths. Just below the low-tide line, the almighty Sunflower Star (p. 112) makes a meal of them. Very young urchins pose a problem with identification, because the baby Purple Sea Urchins are also a pale green, purpling with age.

Red Sea Urchin
STRONGYLOCENTROTUS FRANCISCANUS

Vibrant in color, the Red Sea Urchin, the giant of the West Coast urchins, has spines growing to lengths of 3 inches (7.6 cm). This formidable-looking armory not only serves to protect, but also snares drifting fragments of algae. The algae are then gradually pulled apart and eaten. These scavengers eat all kinds of food, including dead fish, and they are found on open and sheltered rocky shores. At the lowest tides along calm shores, wander down to the water and you might be fortunate enough to witness stunning carpets of the Red Sea Urchin.

RANGE: Alaska to Southern California

ZONE: low-tide line, subtidal to 300 ft (91 m)

HABITATS: rocky shores, open and protected coasts

WIDTH: to 5 in (13 cm) without spines

COLOR: pink, red, reddish-purple

Sea Otters (p. 31) are fond of urchins, and they can be seen pulling them apart on their bellies while floating on their backs. Where otters flourish, the Red Sea Urchin does not. Additional threats to the urchin are people who have developed a fascination for eating their ovaries. Between the spines are tiny pincer-like projections that pinch away at anything venturing too close. These can be enough—but not always—to scare off the hungry attention of a Sunflower Star (p. 112), but are certainly no good against humans.

Purple Sea Urchin
STRONGYLOCENTROTUS PURPURATUS

Gorgeously colored in purple, this vibrant urchin is a spectacle of the exposed rocky coasts where the surf pounds. They are found in tidepools, and there is something of a mystery surrounding these relatives of sea stars and cucumbers. Perhaps with their five teeth, maybe with their sharp spines, many Purple Sea Urchins end up in deep depressions in impossibly hard rock. It appears they erode holes into the rock, and sometimes can never get out of them. Occasionally, they occur in such large numbers that the rock can be riddled with their burrows.

Algae are the main component of their diet, although it is likely that rock is also consumed (not that it has great nutritional value). Senior urchins, sometimes as old as 30 years, enjoy the exposed rocks while the juveniles tend to hide away in small crevices or mussel beds. Young urchins less than 1 inch (2.5 cm) wide have greenish spines, and might be mistaken for the Green Sea Urchin. The Sunflower Star (p. 112) can tolerate the urchin's spiny defense and will make a meal of them.

RANGE: Alaska to Southern California

ZONE: middle to lower intertidal, subtidal to 30 ft (9.1 m)

HABITATS: exposed rocky shores, tidepools

WIDTH: to 3.5 in (8.9 cm) without spines

COLOR: purple (green juvenile)

SIMILAR SPECIES: Green Sea Urchin (p. 115)

Red Sea Cucumber
CUCUMARIA MINIATA

Sea cucumbers are definitely one of the more extraordinary features of the intertidal zone. Somewhat resembling a salad item, they are most definitely animal, and are related to starfish and sea urchins. The Red Sea Cucumber has five rows of tube feet down its length, hinting at the shared ancestry—think of the Bat Star's (p. 110) five arms and the Eccentric Sand Dollar's (p. 114) five-lobed markings. These tube feet help the cucumber lodge into crevices and under rocks at the low-tide line.

When feeding, a fabulous display of 10 crimson, branching tentacles opens up around the mouth. These tentacles filter the seawater for tiny particles of food. Once a tentacle is sufficiently loaded, it is drawn into the mouth and wiped clean. If hassled by enthusiastic beachcombers, the tentacles retract and the whole body stiffens up. Often, the tentacles are all you can see of the buried cucumber. Also burying itself under rocks at the low-tide line is the much smaller White Sea Cucumber (*Eupentacta quinquesemita*). The conspicuous California Stichopus, similar with its reddish tones, has distinctive spines on its body.

RANGE: Alaska to Northern California

ZONE: lower intertidal, subtidal to 80 ft (24 m)

HABITATS: rocky shores, crevices

LENGTH: 10 in (25 cm)

WIDTH: 1 in (2.5 cm)

COLOR: tentacles crimson, body red to purple

SIMILAR SPECIES: California Stichopus (p. 119)

118

California Stichopus
STICHOPUS CALIFORNICUS

Squishy when fully extended, this clumsy-looking character is a likely encounter near the low-tide line of protected rocky coasts. It comes in shades of brown, red or yellow, and is covered in stout, pointed, spiny projections. On the underside are rows of tube feet. Low tidepools and rock crevices are good places to look, but the California Stichopus has become scarcer owing to possible over-fishing—the muscles of the sea cucumber have recently become an attractive commodity on which people dine.

Pale tentacles surrounding the mouth sift through detritus on the seafloor for any nutritious bits and pieces. Itself a victim of the Sunflower Star (p. 112), the California Stichopus tries to avoid this fate—the smell of the sea star sets the cucumber into a rapid walk, like an inchworm's, or it can even swim away with undulations of its body. Failing this, the cucumber will eject its body organs through its mouth, abandoning them presumably so that the predator will dine on these, leaving the cucumber to scurry away and grow new organs.

OTHER NAMES: Giant Sea Cucumber; *Parastichopus californicus*

RANGE: British Columbia to California

ZONE: lower intertidal, subtidal to 300 ft (91 m)

HABITATS: rocks, crevices, pilings, protected coasts

LENGTH: to 16 in (41 cm)

WIDTH: to 2 in (5 cm)

COLOR: variable brown, red, orange, yellow

SIMILAR SPECIES: Red Sea Cucumber (p. 118)

Moon Jelly
AURELIA AURITA

The grace of a swimming Moon Jelly with its translucent and pulsating bell is unsurpassed. Sometimes clouds of this jellyfish drift close to shore and when they do, they are readily washed ashore. After a storm, watch for the amorphous and helpless blob of jelly plumped on the sand. The bell is virtually colorless, but the four horseshoe-shaped gonads are clearly seen in their pastel shades and neatly arranged in the middle of the bell. The jellyfish has a small fringe of tentacles at the edge of the bell.

RANGE: Alaska to Southern California
ZONE: inshore or stranded
HABITATS: pelagic
DIAMETER: to 15 in (38 cm)
COLOR: translucent blue-gray

Tiny nematocysts—individual cells armed with miniature spears and toxins—can cause a mild stinging sensation and rash. While many jellyfish use this technique for capturing their prey, the Moon Jelly has a sticky mucus in which tiny zooplankton get trapped. The Many-ribbed Hydromedusa (*Aequorea aequorea*) is another jellyfish that is frequently washed ashore, but it is smaller and does not have such obvious gonads as the Moon Jelly.

Aggregating Anemone

ANTHOPLEURA ELEGANTISSIMA

Aggregating Anemones can be seen in profusion throughout much of the intertidal zone, smothering rocks in tidepools or isolated rocks on beaches. On surf-pounded beaches look on the sheltered side of rocks protected from the beating waves. When exposed, the elegant blue or pink stinging tentacles are withdrawn, and the anemones appear as greenish blobs of jelly. Sand and gravel often adhere to the body of the anemone in such quantities that the anemones seemingly disappear.

A large aggregation, or colony, is formed by one anemone that has repeatedly divided, or cloned. Two colonies beside each other will have a small gap dividing them, as if they are intolerant of touching each other. When solitary this anemone can reach much larger sizes. The greenish color in the body of the anemone comes from tiny algae that are living in the host's soft tissues. They have a safe haven here, and are thought to provide some nutrition in return. Otherwise, the anemone depends on crustaceans or other small organisms that fail to escape the menacing armored tentacles.

OTHER NAME: Elegant Anemone

RANGE: Alaska to Southern California

ZONE: upper to lower intertidal

HABITATS: rocky shores, tidepools

WIDTH: 2 in (5 cm) closed, 3.5 in (8.9 cm) open

COLOR: green body, variable tentacles

Giant Green Anemone

ANTHOPLEURA XANTHOGRAMMICA

The stunning green form of this huge anemone is hard to miss on the open rocky coasts. Shining away in tidepools and surge channels, this anemone enjoys a rough ride from the waves. Its brilliance comes from a colony of algae growing inside the translucent flesh, where they are provided with a home and offer some nutrition in return. If deprived of light, the algae can die, and the anemone loses its magnificent color. Look on the side of the dark column and foot for tiny Stearn's Sea Spiders (p. 149) quietly sucking away.

The tentacles are armed with tiny cells that each have a miniature harpoon. If you brush your hand across the tentacles they feel sticky, and this sensation is the tiny harpoons trying to drag you in. Once some prey is caught, the tentacles pass it into the mouth in the middle, and the food is then digested. Anything that is not usable is then ejected out of the same hole. These anemones are often positioned where they can catch mussels that have been dislodged by rough surf.

RANGE: Alaska to Southern California

ZONE: lower intertidal, subtidal to 50 ft (15 m)

HABITATS: rocky shores, tidepools, channels

WIDTH: to 10 in (25 cm)

COLOR: variable greenish-blue

Proliferating Anemone
EPIACTIS PROLIFERA

Petite and pretty, these delicate anemones come in a variety of colors in variable shades of red, green and brown. In rocky situations they tend to be pink or red, while on Eelgrass (p. 179) or algae they are green or brown. White stripes radiate from the mouth and mark the column. They can often be found in small gatherings in tidepools and at the base of rocks usually along the open coasts and in bays. They are widespread along much of the Pacific coast.

The odd breeding behavior of this anemone is worth noting. Eggs are fertilized inside the cavity, and then the tiny young move out of the mouth, slide down the side of the anemone, and settle down on the wide column. Here they will stay until they are large enough to fend for themselves. The young don't wander too far, staying close to the parent and forming large patches of individual anemones. This squat anemone is readily eaten by the Leather Star (p. 107) as well as nudibranchs.

OTHER NAME: Brooding Anemone

RANGE: Alaska to Southern California

ZONE: upper to lower intertidal, subtidal to 30 ft (9.1 m)

HABITATS: rocky shores, tidepools, Eelgrass beds, algae

WIDTH: to 2 in (5 cm)

COLOR: variable green, red, brown, pink

Frilled Anemone
METRIDIUM SENILE

At low tide, in quiet waters, be sure to peek into pools or along pilings and seawalls for the beautiful Frilled Anemone. It does occur intertidally, but in quiet corners or under ledges. Calm seas are preferred and subtidally they can grow to enormous sizes. The anemone has a mass of thin cream-colored tentacles, with a richly colored column that is often reddish-brown. The bushy tentacles are used to sweep up tiny floating sea life.

The Frilled Anemone has several ways of going about reproducing. Aside from using an egg and fertilizing it with the male's sperm, the anemone can split down the middle lengthways to create two identical individuals. Even more bizarre is its habit of leaving bits of its foot behind—each one of those bits can generate into a new anemone. The whiff of food is often the primary motive for making an anemone shift from its footing. When wandering around, these anemones defend their own space, readily shooting stinging cells at one another.

OTHER NAME: Plumed Anemone

RANGE: Alaska to Southern California

ZONE: low-tide line, subtidal to 100 ft (30 m)

HABITATS: rocky shores, pilings, tidepools

WIDTH: to 9 in (23 cm)

HEIGHT: to 18 in (46 cm)

COLOR: variable reddish, brown, white

Painted Urticina
URTICINA CRASSICORNIS

A pretty name for a beautiful anemone, the Painted Urticina is hidden away in protected locations near the low-tide line. This anemone comes in many hues, most commonly in shades of red and cream. Approximately 100 tentacles are banded, and deep-colored stripes run between the bases of the tentacles. The stout column and foot are sometimes uniformly colored, but may come blotched in shades of red, cream and green.

This anemone shows up in tidepools, and may be buried in the sand or gravel so that only the stunning crown of tentacles can be seen. This ring of waving projections is seen as certain death by small crabs, sea urchins, snails and some small fish. All of these are heartily enjoyed by the Painted Urticina. Once the prey succumbs to the will of the anemone, it is transferred to the central mouth and down into the body cavity, which serves as one huge stomach. Sometimes you can even see large prey being forced inside the body, doubtlessly to last the hungry anemone some considerable length of time!

OTHER NAME: Northern Red Anemone; *Tealia crassicornis*

RANGE: Alaska to Northern California

ZONE: lower intertidal, subtidal to 100 ft (30 m)

HABITATS: rocky shores, tidepools

WIDTH: to 6 in (15 cm)

HEIGHT: to 5 in (13 cm)

COLOR: variable red, green, cream

Orange Cup Coral

BALANOPHYLLIA ELEGANS

The closest thing we have to the incredible coral reefs of the tropics is this tiny cup coral. The Pacific waters are too rough and cold to support anything more exciting in this region, and intertidally, this is the only coral we will see. A little work is required to see it, because it often prefers the darker overhangs of ledges very close to the low-tide line. Here, it is not at risk of drying out—it is protected from direct sunlight and is uncovered for only a short time.

RANGE: British Columbia to Southern California

ZONE: lower intertidal, subtidal to 160 ft (49 m)

HABITATS: tidepools, crevices, overhangs, open coasts

DIAMETER: to 0.4 in (1 cm) coral cup

COLOR: orange

The Orange Cup Coral, when exposed at low tide, looks like a sharp and calcareous cup with radiating walls inside and a tint of orange. In tidepools the delicate translucent creature emerges from its stony home, spreading its faintly orange tentacles to catch and sting small prey. This coral is related to sea anemones, differing in that it builds a solid coral base to withdraw into. Other cup corals can be found at greater depths, but well out of reach of the beachcomber.

Red Crab
CANCER PRODUCTUS

When lifting rocks at low tide, you might well be struck by the stunning, deeply colored Red Crab. This crab is commonly found from quiet bays to exposed coasts. Distinctive features include the rounded 'teeth' bordering the edge of its wide carapace and black tips to its pincers. If these pincers don't put you off, gently have a look at the underside for the soft creamy yellow colors. Keep in mind that the pincers are strong enough to crack through a shell!

The Oregon Cancer Crab (*C. oregonensis*) is a much smaller and rounder crab that might be confused with young Red Crabs, which are a real treat to find. The variable colors of juvenile Red Crabs can be anything from red to white, blue to orange, with a carapace frequently etched with elaborate markings like an intricate maze. As they mature, they can rest in the knowledge that they will not be facing a similar fate as the Dungeness Crab, frequently seen on our dinner plates; Red Crabs have a shell that is just too thick.

RANGE: Alaska to Southern California

ZONE: low-tide line, subtidal to 300 ft (91 m)

HABITATS: sounds, bays, Eelgrass beds, rocky shores, tidepools

WIDTH: carapace to 6.25 in (15.9 cm)

LENGTH: carapace to 4.25 in (10.8 cm)

COLOR: deep reds

SIMILAR SPECIES: Dungeness Crab (p. 128)

Dungeness Crab
CANCER MAGISTER

I n spring you might be surprised to find countless crab shells on sandy beaches. These gray-brown, fan-shaped carapaces are not dead crabs, but the discards of the living. Look for 10 sharp 'teeth' along the edge, the tenth marking the widest point of the carapace. Each crab will molt up to 15 times in its life. Molting is the precursor to the prolonged embrace of a male and female and the production of copious quantities of eggs.

The Dungeness Crab prefers sandy offshore waters, but younger crabs can be found in the intertidal zone, lurking in Eelgrass (p. 179) or in the bottom of sandy tidepools. By day the crabs bury themselves with only their eyes protruding above the sand. This crab prefers to chip away at clams with its stout pale pincers, while it in turn is cracked open by people. A popular commercial catch, the Dungeness Crab is offered protection from exploitation, because only male crabs 6.5 inches (17 cm) or larger can be taken. Males have a narrower abdominal flap than the female, rather like a curled under tail.

OTHER NAME: Pacific Edible Crab

RANGE: Alaska to Southern California

ZONE: lower intertidal, subtidal to 755 ft (230 m)

HABITATS: estuaries, bays, Eelgrass beds, sandy tidepools

WIDTH: carapace to 9.25 in (23.5 cm)

LENGTH: carapace to 6.4 in (16.3 cm)

COLOR: gray-brown, purple tint

SIMILAR SPECIES: Red Crab (p. 127)

Purple Shore Crab

HEMIGRAPSUS NUDUS

The Purple Shore Crab is a feisty and aggressive little resident of the high and middle reaches of the intertidal zone. Often hiding under rocks by day, this crab can be identified by its deep purple color (but it also comes reddish-brown or green), and it is distinctive for the pretty purple dots on the pincers. Three small 'teeth' define the edge of the carapace behind the eyes.

Very common intertidally, the Purple Shore Crab can be found from the wave-swept rocky shores to the calm waters of estuaries. Mussel beds, crevices and underneath rocks are the nooks where it will hide by day. By night at low tide they emerge to scavenge and feed on bits of algae, sometimes venturing onto sandy beaches. Despite their herbivorous habits, they are defensive and will happily nip at you. In the quiet waters of estuaries and sounds, this crab will often share space with the Yellow Shore Crab (*H. oregonensis*). This paler and hairier version of the Purple Shore Crab prefers muddy areas.

RANGE: Alaska to Southern California

ZONE: intertidal

HABITATS: rocky shores, estuaries, under rocks

WIDTH: carapace to 2.25 in (5.7 cm)

LENGTH: carapace to 2 in (5 cm)

COLOR: variable purple, reddish-brown, olive-green

SIMILAR SPECIES: Black-clawed Mud Crab (p. 130)

Black-clawed Mud Crab

LOPHOPANOPEUS BELLUS

Where gravel and sand combine, turn over larger rocks to reveal the Black-clawed Mud Crab. These pebble-sized crabs think they are much larger, and they will raise their black-tipped claws to ward off any naturalists that get too close. If you decide to ignore this aggressive posture, pick the crab up and it will play dead. Colors of this crab are very variable, coming in plain and mottled hues of brown, red or purple among others. The purple version might well be confused with the Purple Shore Crab, so be sure to look at its other features. The black-tipped pincers are a dead give-away.

The fan-shaped carapace has three prominent 'teeth' at the front corners. The chunky pincers pick apart all kinds of matter—this crab scavenges for bits and pieces of both plants and animals. Tucked away near the low-tide line, these crabs show up on rocky shores and in estuaries and bays, especially in tidepools and under algal holdfasts. Unlike most crabs, the female can mate when she has a hard shell—others have to molt.

OTHER NAME: Black-clawed Pebble Crab

RANGE: Alaska to Northern California

ZONE: lower intertidal, subtidal to 240 ft (73 m)

HABITATS: estuaries, bays, rocks, cobbles, tidepools, algal holdfasts

WIDTH: to 1.4 in (3.6 cm)

LENGTH: 1 in (2.5 cm)

COLOR: very variable, brown, red, purple, green

SIMILAR SPECIES: Purple Shore Crab (p. 129)

Flat Porcelain Crab

PETROLISTHES CINCTIPES

When you turn rocks on beaches, the tiny crabs that scuttle away are likely to be Flat Porcelain Crabs. These crabs have a rounded carapace barely 1 inch (2.5 cm) in length, and they are usually quite drab in their various shades of brown (and occasionally blue). The long antennae are a deep red, and the claws seem enormous compared to the size of the body. In counting the legs you will discover it has only four pairs, while most 'true' crabs have five pairs. Porcelain Crabs are filter feeders, sifting through the water for tiny and nutritious particles of food.

These crabs are very flat, which is an advantage when trying to squeeze into crevices or nooks on rocks or beds of California Mussel (p. 90). If a crab fails to tuck away into a protected niche and is caught by a limb, it will happily autotomize, or shed, that leg in order to escape. The lost leg will soon regrow, so it is not a major loss to the crab. The crab's apparent brittleness gave it its 'porcelain' name.

RANGE: British Columbia to Southern California

ZONE: upper to middle intertidal

HABITATS: under rocks, stones, mussel beds

LENGTH: carapace to 1 in (2.5 cm)

COLOR: browns

Shield-backed Kelp Crab

PUGETTIA PRODUCTA

This is an elegant crab with an attitude, so if you are tempted to pick one up, be warned, because the long legs and claws can reach much further than the average crab. The smooth but sharply spined carapace comes in various shades to match the seaweed on which the crab lives and dines—olive-green to reddish-brown shades are flecked with darker spots. Long limbs help the crab grasp onto swaying kelp fronds. Watch for these crabs grasping fronds of seaweed washing back and forth in the surf. Sometimes an orange-brown crab will turn up in emerald surfgrass, in striking contrast.

The younger Shield-backed Kelp Crabs are intertidal, hidden under rocks and in tidepools. As they age, they tend to move into deeper water and the kelp beds. In summer they will dine on kelp, but in winter, when much of the kelp has died, they become carnivores, extending their diet to barnacles and other intertidal organisms. The Sharp-nosed Crab (*Scyra acutifrons*) is smaller and tends to stick seaweed onto its spiky nose to help it blend in.

RANGE: Alaska to Southern California

ZONE: low intertidal, subtidal to 240 ft (73 m)

HABITATS: rocky shores, kelp beds, tidepools, rocks

WIDTH: to 3.75 in (9.5 cm)

LENGTH: to 4.75 in (12 cm)

COLOR: variable reddish-brown to olive-green

132

Blue-handed Hermit Crab

PAGURUS SAMUELIS

H ermit crabs are one of the most popular intertidal animals with their unusual preference for living in snail shells, and their shy habit of hiding away. One of the commonest hermit crabs to be found is the Blue-handed Hermit Crab, the adults of which show a distinct preference for shells of the Black Tegula (p. 68). This hermit is olive to yellowish-green in color, and most distinct are the bright blue bands around the base of the legs. Its antennae are bright red.

The carapace is striped and ends as a beak-like projection between the eyes. This projection and the bright blue band distinguish this hermit from the Grainy Hermit Crab (*P. granosimanus*), which is found lower in the intertidal zone. Hermit crabs have soft abdomens that they need to tuck away inside shells for protection. At the end is a hook-like tail that clings to the inside of the shell. As they grow, they need to move into a larger shell. House moving must be done quickly—the crabs are very vulnerable to attack at moving time.

OTHER NAME: Blueband Hermit

RANGE: Alaska to Southern California

ZONE: upper to lower intertidal, subtidal to 50 ft (15 m)

HABITATS: open rocky shores, tidepools

LENGTH: to 0.75 in (1.9 cm)

COLOR: olive-green to yellowish, blue bands

SIMILAR SPECIES: Hairy Hermit Crab (p. 134)

Hairy Hermit Crab
PAGURUS HIRSUTIUSCULUS

Unlike the Blue-handed Hermit Crab or the Grainy Hermit Crab (*P. granosimanus*), the Hairy Hermit Crab is noticeably hairy. On some of the legs there are white and blue bands, but they are not as striking as with the Blue-handed Hermit Crab. The long gray-green antennae are flecked with white dots. The shells this hermit chooses, often dogwinkles and whelks, never seem large enough, and the crab cannot withdraw all the way in. The Hairy is a very common hermit crab of upper tidepools and is the most common one in Puget Sound. The Grainy Hermit Crab occurs at lower levels.

RANGE: Alaska to Southern California

ZONE: upper to middle intertidal

HABITATS: tidepools, rocky shores, open and protected coasts

LENGTH: to 0.75 in (1.9 cm)

COLOR: gray-green, banded legs

SIMILAR SPECIES: Blue-handed Hermit Crab (p. 133)

If picked up, the Hairy Hermit Crab readily drops out of its shell, and then has to run in search of a replacement. For some reason this behavior is not demonstrated so much on the open coast as it is in quiet waters. This hermit, like others, is a scavenger for bits of plants and animals. In upper tidepools, large congregations can often be seen gathered around stranded seaweed. Sensitive to the approach of a naturalist, they will quickly withdraw into their shells, and tumble down to the bottom of the tidepool.

Acorn Barnacle

BALANUS GLANDULA

By far one of the most abundant animals to be found on rocky shores, these inconspicuous barnacles are easy to step over and ignore. Bend down a moment and study them! The Acorn Barnacle prefers the middle to upper intertidal zone where it is out of reach of predatory *Nucella* snails (pp. 52–54). So tolerant are barnacles that an occasional ocean spray keeps them alive. During scorching sun or heavy rain, these tiny crustaceans, which are related to crabs and shrimps, close up their impenetrable plates like doors.

OTHER NAME: Common Barnacle

RANGE: Alaska to Southern California

ZONE: upper to middle intertidal

HABITATS: rocky shores

DIAMETER: 0.6 in (1.5 cm)

COLOR: gray-white

SIMILAR SPECIES: Thatched Barnacle (p. 137)

The Small Acorn Barnacle (*Chthamalus dalli*) is only 0.1 inch (2.5 mm) across and is often seen growing next to the larger and paler Acorn Barnacle. The protective plates inside the 'crater' help identify which species you are looking at: the Small Acorn Barnacle has a religious cross while the Acorn Barnacle has wavy edges. As the tide recedes, be sure to look into small tidepools filled with barnacles, and watch for their frantically waving cirri—these are hand-like projections—that grasp for any tiny food particles left by the receding waters.

Giant Acorn Barnacle

BALANUS NUBILUS

Near the low-tide line of open coasts, it is possible to see this massive barnacle adhered to rocks, pilings or other hard surfaces. So large is this barnacle that it was roasted by the aboriginal peoples of the Northwest to eat. Sometimes the barnacles grow in bunches, on top of one another, until the mass becomes so thick and unstable that a storm can break it off at the base.

RANGE: Alaska to Southern California

ZONE: lower intertidal, subtidal to 300 ft (91 m)

HABITATS: rocky shores, exposed coasts

DIAMETER: to 4 in (10 cm)

COLOR: gray-white plates, pinkish flesh

Each barnacle is made from rough outer plates that are frequently encrusted with many different organisms. The inner plates are pointed and protect the cirri (hand-like projections) that come out to catch particles of food when the tide is in.

A barnacle is much like a shrimp that has landed on its head and built a wall around itself. This barnacle is almost as high as it is wide, and when the animal dies, the cavity left behind makes an ideal home for many organisms. Crabs such as the Oregon Cancer Crab (*Cancer oregonensis*) will hide away inside, as will the delightful Grunt Sculpin (p. 42).

Thatched Barnacle
SEMIBALANUS CARIOSUS

Closer to the low-tide line the Thatched Barnacle becomes the dominant species of barnacle. This crustacean grows to 2 inches (5 cm) across its base, and is almost as tall when it is on its own. In a group, however, they can be so tightly packed that they grow very tall and thin, looking more like pencils. This happens in the north of their range more than in the south, and in some places there can be as many as 12,540 per square yard (15,000 per sq. m)!

Rocky shores or other firm surfaces are required for this barnacle to set up home. As the barnacle grows, it puts down thread-like calcareous deposits that give a unique, ridged appearance to the barnacle. It is this texture that has earned it the name of Thatched Barnacle. The Acorn Barnacle is similar but smaller and lacks the characteristic ridges spilling down the side like lava flows. These are long-lived creatures, some as much as 15 years old. However, many fall prey to the hungry Ochre Sea Star (p. 111), never attaining such a grand old age.

RANGE: Alaska to Southern California

ZONE: middle to lower intertidal

HABITATS: rocky shores

DIAMETER: to 2 in (5 cm)

COLOR: gray-white

SIMILAR SPECIES: Acorn Barnacle (p. 135)

Common Goose Barnacle

LEPAS ANATIFERA

After a violent storm, be sure to hike the sandy beaches for articles that have drifted in from the high seas. Aside from disheartening garbage, there is often driftwood sculpted by years in the ocean. Inside the wood are many Pacific Shipworms (p. 77), and outside are the strange Common Goose Barnacles. These creatures can be found in large colonies on anything that has been floating in the sea, including plastic and styrofoam. The tiny nauplius (barnacle larva) swims in open waters until attracted to the shade of something floating— here it sticks for good.

Common Goose Barnacles might not look like the barnacles stuck on rock, but they are closely related. A thick fleshy stalk supports the crustacean. Smooth, white plates form a shell surrounding the rest of the animal's body, and when submerged, the cirri (hand-like projections) are extended out to filter the water with fine hairs. Each plate is bordered in yellow. When these barnacles drift onto the shore, baking sunshine soon kills them, and the gasping barnacle can be seen hanging out of its home.

OTHER NAME: Pelagic Goose Barnacle

RANGE: Alaska to Southern California

ZONE: high-tide line

HABITATS: pelagic, on floats

LENGTH: to 6 in (15 cm)

COLOR: black stalk, white shell

SIMILAR SPECIES: Leaf Barnacle (p. 139)

Leaf Barnacle
POLLICIPES POLYMERUS

In thick clusters stuck amidst California Mussel beds (p. 90) of the exposed coast, Leaf Barnacles are frequently found. These peculiar bunches of crustaceans thrive in the pounding surf—surge channels and very exposed rocks being the favored locations. They differ from the Common Goose Barnacle in that they stick to rocks on shore, and have many smaller plates protecting the animal inside. The stalk is a deep reddish-black and covered in miniscule spines arranged in neat rows. These stalks are tough and rubbery to cope with the stress of stormy seas.

As waves break over the rocks, the barnacles open and stretch out their cirri to catch the backwash off the rocks.

OTHER NAME: Goose Barnacle

RANGE: British Columbia to Southern California

ZONE: upper to lower intertidal

HABITATS: rocky shores, mussel beds

LENGTH: to 3.25 in (8.3 cm)

COLOR: dark stalk, whitish plates

SIMILAR SPECIES: Common Goose Barnacle (p. 138)

Their hope is to rake in any small organisms washed off their footings. When closed, dark red 'lips' mark where the cirri come out. If you pass your hand over the top so that your shadow passes over them, notice how they twist and retract a little bit. Why they do this is a mystery, but obviously they are light sensitive.

Smooth Skeleton Shrimp

CAPRELLA LAEVIUSCULA

The peculiar and rakish Smooth Skeleton Shrimp clings to hydroids, algae and Eelgrass (p. 179) in both rocky and sandy shores. The last three pairs of legs have hooks for feet, and these hooks help the creature grasp tightly and securely to its perch. From here it waves gently back and forth, consuming tiny animals suspended in the water, pieces of algae and single-celled plants.

Although it carries the name 'shrimp,' it is not a true shrimp, but belongs to a group of crustaceans called amphipods. The highly jointed body bears numerous appendages and claws, and it comes in shades of green, tan or pinkish, depending on which color best suits the location for camouflage.

Occasionally, skeleton shrimps, of which there are a number of different species, can be seen clinging in clusters together with their arms outstretched. Like strange beasts from another planet, these animals deserve some close inspection with a hand lens so that you can see their strange body shape and curious behavior.

RANGE: British Columbia to Southern California

ZONE: lower intertidal, shallow subtidal

HABITATS: Eelgrass beds, algae, hydroids, rocky and sandy areas

LENGTH: to 2 in (5 cm)

COLOR: variable green, tan, pinkish

Vosnesensky's Isopod

IDOTEA WOSNESENSKII

An isopod is a type of crustacean and Vosnesensky was a Russian zoologist who collected these appealing creatures in the 19th century—together they give this species a name that seems more appropriate for a small spaceship. These creatures are most often green, but will assume many colors to help them blend with the background. Most stunning are the isopods found on encrusting algae, in various shades of mottled pink. Black, red and brown versions also occur.

Tucked away under rocks by day, they venture out at night and can be seen swimming across tidepools. Where there are accumulations of rotting seaweed, there is a higher chance of encountering the flattened isopod and its seven pairs of legs. Mussel beds provide plenty of cover for them, too. Similar but gray and smaller is the Stubby Isopod (*Gnorimosphaeroma oregonense*), which can be found in profusion in some places, especially where fresh water seeps. The Stubby Isopod is characterized by its ability to curl up into a tight ball, much like terrestrial pill bugs.

OTHER NAME: Rockweed Isopod

RANGE: Alaska to Southern California

ZONE: upper to lower intertidal, subtidal to 53 ft (16 m)

HABITATS: exposed, quiet rocky shores, mussel beds, seaweed, tidepools

LENGTH: to 1.4 in (3.6 cm)

COLOR: very variable, green, pink, brown, red, black

California Beach Flea

MEGALORCHESTIA CALIFORNIANA

Amidst the wrack cast up on beaches at the high-tide line, thousands of small jumping creatures are tucked away. On exposed sandy beaches most of these creatures are the California Beach Fleas. By day they rest and keep moist either in their burrows or under mats of kelp decomposing on the shore. By night, they come out in the thousands to feast on the latest kelp delivery from the sea. The beach fleas follow the waves down the beach, and retreat before the tide comes in.

With a sandy-colored body and bright red antennae, these are attractive crustaceans. Younger individuals have darker patches down their back. Unfortunately, many people are put off by the sheer number of fleas and their writhing jumping madness when disturbed. That they are called fleas doesn't help at all, because California Beach Fleas do not bite. Strong back legs give them an enormous athletic talent for jumping, and it is for this that they have earned their common name. A smaller and drabber version is the Beach Hopper (*Traskorchestia traskiana*) of bays and quieter beaches.

OTHER NAME: *Orchestoidea californiana*

RANGE: British Columbia to Southern California

ZONE: high-tide line and above

HABITATS: sandy beaches

LENGTH: to 1.1 in (2.8 cm)

COLOR: tan, red antennae

Coon-stripe Shrimp

PANDALUS DANAE

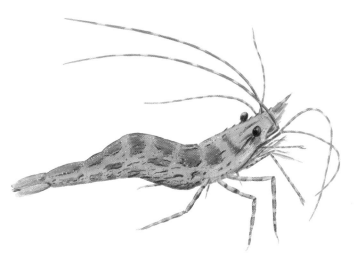

From time to time, frisky shrimp can be seen in tidepools near the low-tide line. The commonest shrimps are the Broken-back Shrimps of the *Heptacarpus* genus, with their distinctive kink in the back. Occasionally, though, you may be lucky to see the brightly colored Coon-stripe Shrimp. Younger, smaller shrimp will frequent tidepools and often hide in seaweed. They are mostly reddish and tan, with stripes of brown and dots of white and blue. The long antennae and legs are banded in brown and red. Coloration will vary from one individual to the next.

When caught subtidally, these shrimp are larger than the tidepool residents, and make up a major part of the shrimp industry, frequently showing up in markets. For many years fishermen wondered why females were so much larger than males, until it was discovered that these shrimp are male when they are young and small, becoming female as they get older. In addition to tidepools, both males and females turn up in quiet bays and estuaries, as well as in beds of Eelgrass (p. 179) and around dock pilings.

OTHER NAME: Dock Shrimp

RANGE: Alaska to Northern California

ZONE: lower intertidal, subtidal to 600 ft (183 m)

HABITATS: rocky shores to muddy sand, tidepools, pilings

LENGTH: to 6 in (15 cm)

COLOR: reddish, tan, dark stripes

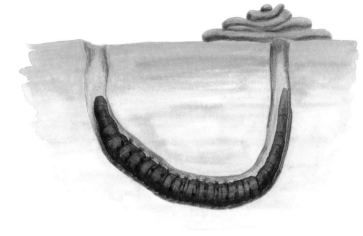

If you are perusing the muddy sands of quiet bays, Lug Worm evidence is unmistakable. While the worm is seldom seen, fecal castings are found in profusion on the surface of the mud. Beneath each one is an ugly worm actively consuming the mud in which it lives. Once all the nutrients are extracted, unwanted mud is excreted onto the surface. Watch a casting for a while and it may just get larger.

Lug Worms live in J-shaped or U-shaped burrows. In J-shaped burrows, the head is pointing down to the bottom. Different segments of the worm's body contract to draw down fresh water, which delivers oxygen to the worm so that it can breathe, as well as fresh particles of sand and mud on which to feed. Along each side of the brown body are numerous hairy projections that serve as the gills. At first glance, there is nothing glamorous about the Lug Worm, but wash off the mud, and it, too, does have some beauty—the gills are often a bright red from the blood surging through them.

RANGE: Alaska to Northern California
ZONE: middle to lower intertidal
HABITATS: muddy sand, quiet bays
LENGTH: to 6 in (15 cm)
COLOR: light to dark brown

Fifteen-scaled Worm

HARMOTHOE IMBRICATA

This strange armored creature inhabits many corners of the inter-tidal zone, tucked away under algal holdfasts or under tidepool rocks. It is very hardy, enjoying all kinds of conditions from the low salinity waters of estuaries to the bitterly cold and dark depths of 11,000 feet (3353 m). This worm, with 15 pairs of scales running down each side, also turns up in the tubes of other worms and the shells of hermit crabs. Its color varies enormously from red to black to green, with additional markings of dots or stripes. Commonest is the gray-green form.

The scales down the back serve as a brooding chamber for the eggs, which are very easily dislodged, so be careful if you are inclined to handle such creatures. They are carnivores and rather intolerant of their own kind— if confined in the same container, some scale worms will readily bite each other. Very similar and found in the same habitats is the Twelve-scaled Worm (*Lepidonotus squamatus*), which grows to the same size. Much larger at over 4 inches (10 cm) is the Eighteen-scaled Worm (*Halosydna brevitosa*).

RANGE: Alaska to Southern California

ZONE: lower intertidal, subtidal to 11,000 ft (3353 m)

HABITATS: tidepools, under rocks, holdfasts, estuaries, open shores, mussel beds

LENGTH: to 2.5 in (6.4 cm)

COLOR: gray-green, highly variable to red, yellow, black

Red Tube Worm
SERPULA VERMICULARIS

When you turn rocks at low tide, you might overlook a dead-looking crusty tube. This calcareous tube, often covered with marine growth, is home to the Red Tube Worm, and is well worth further investigation. When immersed in water, a brilliant display of red gills is pushed out of the sinuous tube. There are 40 pairs of gills with which the worm feeds and breathes. The body of the worm is tucked safely away inside. Some worms have pink gills; others are banded in white.

OTHER NAME: Calcareous Tube Worm

RANGE: Alaska to Southern California

ZONE: lower intertidal to 300 ft (91 m)

HABITATS: under rocks, shells, pilings

LENGTH: to 4 in (10 cm)

COLOR: red, pink, whitish gills

Any firm surface covered with water makes a good home, and the distinctive tubes turn up on pilings and shells. When the feeding worm is disturbed, the gills are withdrawn in a flash, and the entrance to the tube sealed off with a red funnel-shaped operculum. Empty tubes are obvious because they lack this bright red door. Similar but miniscule by comparison is the Tiny Tube Worm (*Spirorbis borealis*), which is commonly found on hard surfaces immersed in water and grows to a mere eighth of an inch (0.3 cm).

Curly Terebellid Worm

THELEPUS CRISPUS

A number of worms have the habit of burying their soft and vulnerable bodies in the sand and gravel, and coating themselves in a wall of mucus and grit. Most common is the Curly Terebellid Worm found on rocky and gravelly shores, sometimes under rocks or peaking out of crevices. The top part of the tube protrudes from the sand and is very tough. Grit and small stones stick to the mucus, which then hardens. The tube is tough enough to withstand the rough life on the open coast. Concealed inside is a long reddish worm that grows to 6 inches (15 cm) in length and up to 11 inches (28 cm) exceptionally.

Out of the top of the tube come translucent pinkish tentacles and some thin reddish gills. The tentacles can reach 12 inches (30 cm) in length, and gently pick their way about the surface collecting tiny particles of food. When disturbed they are withdrawn quickly, but they can break off. In such an event, the tentacles continue to writhe around on their own, in a similar vein to a beheaded chicken.

OTHER NAME: Spaghetti Worm

RANGE: Alaska to Southern California

ZONE: middle to lower intertidal, subtidal to 50 ft (15 m)

HABITATS: rocky, gravelly shores, sand, open coasts

LENGTH: to 11 in (28 cm)

COLOR: pinkish tentacles, reddish body

Six-lined Nemertean

TUBULANUS SEXLINEATUS

This nemertean, or ribbon worm, is an unusual but delightful find among mussel beds, algal growths or other well-covered rocky surfaces in which it can crawl about. Its soft chocolate-brown body is stylishly marked with six white lines running its length, with many white lines around its girth. These worms can be enormously long, stretching out to 3.3 feet (1 m), yet only 8 inches (20 cm) when contracted. Despite this elasticity, it is very fragile, so please do not tug at it because it may just fall apart in your hands!

Like all nemerteans, it is a carnivore, and it has the disturbing habit of reversing its proboscis out of its head to catch its prey. By squeezing a few muscles here and there, the pressure forces the sticky mouthpart out onto the prey. Armed with small arrows and venom, the prey is caught by the proboscis, and then usually swallowed whole. Another giant stretchy ribbon worm is the Orange Nemertean (*T. polymorphus*). This one stretches to even greater lengths and is brightly colored, usually in orange.

RANGE: Alaska to Southern California

ZONE: lower intertidal, subtidal

HABITATS: mussel beds, rocks, algae

LENGTH: stretchy to 3.3 ft (1 m)

COLOR: brown, with white stripes

Stearn's Sea Spider

PYCNOGONUM STEARNSI

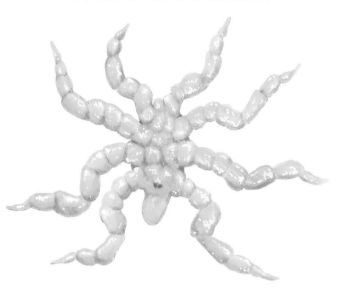

Small and peculiar, the Sea Spider, which is not a spider at all, looks fit for casting in a horror film. Eight legs give it the sinister flair associated with spiders, hence its name, but it is in fact a Pycnogonid. This small creature is all legs. Its abdomen is almost nonexistent, and most of the head is a stout proboscis that it inserts into its prey, and then it sucks out the victim's juices. Small but distinct eyes are set just behind the proboscis. Stearn's Sea Spider comes in gentle shades of yellow to pink.

RANGE:	Alaska to Northern California
ZONE:	middle to lower intertidal
HABITATS:	tidepools, rocks, anemones, tunicates
LENGTH:	0.5 in (1.3 cm)
COLOR:	yellow to pink

If you are determined to find a sea spider, a good source location is the base and column of the Giant Green Anemone (p. 122). Here, small gatherings can be observed feeding. Other anemones also fall prey to these suckers. The Clawed Sea Spider (*Phoxichilidium femoratum*) grows to only 0.1 inch (2.5 mm) in length, but has comparatively long legs. The Clawed Sea Spider is so small you are sure to miss it. Sea spiders are a role model for modern times: the male looks after and carries the eggs until they hatch.

Kelp Encrusting Bryozoan

MEMBRANIPORA MEMBRANACEA

Storm-tossed kelp may not be the first place you might think to look for mysterious marine organisms, but be sure to pick through some Bull Kelp (p. 162) or Giant Perennial Kelp (p. 161). Closely hugging the surface of the algae, you might just find distinctive pale, delicate mats— lacy filigrees of calcareous walls surrounding hundreds of tiny organisms. These are the Kelp Encrusting Bryozoans. Bryozoans come in so many shapes and sizes, some resembling mossy mats, others looking like branching corals.

OTHER NAME: Lacy-crust Bryozoan

RANGE: Alaska to Southern California

ZONE: subtidal

HABITATS: kelp

COLONY SIZE: variable to several inches (cm)

COLOR: white, cream, gray

Each white patch is a whole colony of animals that resemble miniature anemones, with their circular hand of food-catching tentacles. Tiny walls house and separate each individual bryozoan, and the colony expands from the middle outwards, often giving them a round formation. Close inspection in a tub of water with a hand lens is worthwhile, because the tiny creatures will emerge from their protective homes to feed. Look out for a small patch of jelly-like substance that matches the bryozoan colors perfectly— you may be looking at the 0.6-inch (1.5-cm) long Doridella Sea Slug (*Doridella steinbergae*). It browses exclusively on this bryozoan.

Staghorn Bryozoan
HETEROPORA MAGNA

Bryozoans are flat, such as the Kelp Encrusting Bryozoan (p. 150), bushy like miniature trees, and shaggy like clumps of moss. Others resemble garlands of feathers or convincingly resemble branching corals. The Staghorn Bryozoan, found on rocky open coasts, is one such colony of tiny animals that is often mistaken for a coral. From British Columbia to Oregon, however, only one species of coral will likely be encountered, the Orange Cup Coral (p. 126).

This tight-knit community of animals grows in branching columns, the skeleton of the structure being made of calcareous deposits put down by each little zooid. Each zooid is only a fraction of an inch long, and will require a microscope or powerful hand lens to view it. Look closely at the branches of the bryozoan colony to see how beautifully geometric nature can be. Under close inspection, a crown of tentacles can be seen catching tiny single-celled plants and bacteria. Because these are small creatures unable to run away, they make easy eating and are readily consumed by some limpets, chitons and nudibranchs amongst others.

RANGE: British Columbia to Oregon

ZONE: lower intertidal, subtidal

HABITATS: rocky shores, open coasts

COLONY SIZE: variable to 4 in (10 cm)

COLOR: gray, green, cream

Boring Sponge
CLIONA CELATA

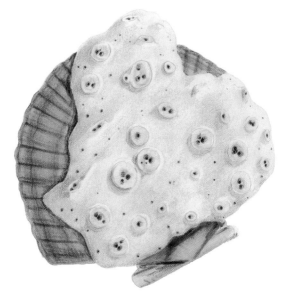

With a somewhat misleading name, this yellow sponge actually has an interesting story to tell. Usually found growing on barnacles and shells, especially the Giant Rock Scallop (p. 76), clams and oysters, the Boring Sponge is a small recycling depot. Special cells secrete sulfuric acid that eats away at the calcium carbonate that makes up shells. This process creates a honeycomb of channels and the shell eventually disintegrates. Dead shells are just as good as the living, and the sponge helps keep the sea from clogging up with piles of abandoned shells.

RANGE: Alaska to Southern California

ZONE: intertidal and subtidal to 400 ft (122 m)

HABITATS: shells, barnacles

DIAMETER: to 12 in (30 cm)

COLOR: yellow

The compounds that make up the shells are then recycled back into the marine system and are once again available for use by other animals—perhaps even by another snail carefully crafting its mobile palace.

The sponge appears as small yellow dots and pores on the shell surface, until it grows so large that it can completely smother the host. While beachcombing, be sure to study the shell fragments for the small holes and honeycomb matrix that the sponge leaves behind.

Purple Sponge
HALICLONA PERMOLLIS

Soft, smooth and purple, these sponges may not seem to be animals, but they are, albeit primitive. The gorgeously colored Purple Sponge is found encrusting hard surfaces in calmer waters and tidepools. Close inspection will reveal tiny holes in the surface. Really small holes are incurrent holes, inside of which are small cells with beating flagella on them that draw in water. The large holes, which resemble volcanoes, are called 'oscula,' and it is from these that water flows out.

Sponges are not the most dynamic of animals, their attractive colors being one of the few things that make them stand out. Pretty much all they do is pump water through the extensive matrix, sifting it for microscopic particles on which they dine. The matrix is supported by tiny spicules made of silica, or glass, and hungry sea slugs put these to use in their own skin. One such hungry sea slug is the Ring-spotted Doris (p. 101). The similar gray-green Crumb-of-bread Sponge (*Halichondria panicea*) has a texture like bread, and is found in the same range and further to the north.

RANGE: Washington to Northern California

ZONE: middle to lower intertidal, subtidal to 20 ft (6.1 m)

HABITATS: hard surfaces, protected shores

DIAMETER: to 36 in (91 cm)

COLOR: pink to purple

Velvety Red Sponge

OPHLITASPONGIA PENNATA

Vibrant splashes of red splashed about on rocks are most likely from the brilliant Velvety Red Sponge. This common sponge prefers the open coasts but seeks out overhangs and darker crevices. Encrusting and very flat, it occurs from the middle intertidal zone down to subtidal waters. As its name implies, it is soft and velvety to the touch, and tiny pores pockmark its entire surface.

Get down on your hands and knees to observe the sponge closely, because on most large patches, it is guarding a little secret. As illustrated, you may be able to make out the tiny and adorable Crimson Doris (*Rostanga pulchra*). This sea slug matches the sponge's color to perfection, thus making it hard to notice. The little slug seldom wanders from the sponge that it feeds and lays its eggs on—if it did the slug would become obvious because of its dazzling color. The Crimson Doris barely grows to half an inch (1.27 cm) in length. Eggs, also bright red, are laid in little coils on the sponge.

RANGE: British Columbia to Southern California

ZONE: middle intertidal to shallow subtidal

HABITATS: rocks, dark crevices, open coasts

DIAMETER: to 36 in (91 cm)

COLOR: red

Sea Pork
APLIDIUM SPP.

For those with a bit of imagination, colonies of these encrusting animals may look like a slab of pork. Sea Pork is a low-growing mass of tunicates, or sea squirts. These are filter feeders, with an intake and outlet for water to pass through, and they favor very clean water. Where wave action is strong it is possible to see these creatures.

Sea squirts come in various shapes and sizes, and the Sea Pork is a colonial form, of which there are many different species determined in part by color. Sea Porks usually come in pinkish hues, but white and brown are common shades.

RANGE: Alaska to California

ZONE: lower intertidal, subtidal to 1200 ft (366 m)

HABITATS: wave-washed rocks, open coasts

DIAMETER: to 8 in (20 cm)

COLOR: variable, white, pink, brown

These colonies are smooth to the touch, and resemble some sponges, but there the similarity ends. Sea squirts are sophisticated equivalents of sponges, but are not related to them. Sea spiders can sometimes be found sticking their mouths in and feeding on them, and the Oregon Triton (p. 59) favors an occasional meal of Sea Pork. Food for the Sea Pork is the microscopic component of the water that it filters—bacteria and single-celled plants and animals.

Monterey Stalked Tunicate

STYELA MONTEREYENSIS

This tunicate is distinctive for its long stalk and tough body with two valves, or siphons, at the top. It is a solitary tunicate, unlike the large colonies of Sea Pork (p. 155), and it can often be found suspended from overhangs in quieter corners of surge channels. The protected side of rocks on exposed coasts is favored, and pilings where the water is clean may harbor several individuals. The main body of the animal is wrinkled longitudinally, and the texture is tough and almost woody. The color varies from yellowish to red-brown. Sometimes the tunicate is covered with other organisms, although this seldom happens when it is growing where there are swift currents.

OTHER NAME: Stalked Sea Squirt

RANGE: Southern British Columbia to California

ZONE: lower intertidal, subtidal to 100 ft (30 m)

HABITATS: surge channels, rocks, open and protected coasts, pilings

HEIGHT: to 10 in (25 cm)

COLOR: tan to red-brown

Surprisingly, we have quite a lot in common with sea squirts. A free-swimming larval tunicate has a primitive spinal cord, a stomach and a heart, and is not unlike a human when first developing. As they age, though, this resemblance fades and the cord disappears. As the larva grows, it decides to settle down on a rock, taking on its new adult form.

Wrinkled Sea Squirt

PYURA HAUSTOR

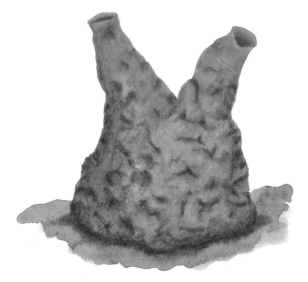

Careful scrutiny is required to notice this stumpy solitary tunicate. Its tough and knobby skin is more often than not covered in bits of shell and other marine debris, and will be colonized by many other organisms. Often, all that can be seen are the two bright red lips of the siphons peeking out of a mass of marine growth. At the low-tide line, look among rocks of the open coast and on pilings in protected waters. Sometimes they are tightly packed into a mussel bed. South of Oregon, they are strictly subtidal.

OTHER NAME: Warty Sea Squirt

RANGE: Alaska to Oregon

ZONE: lower intertidal, subtidal to 660 ft (201 m)

HABITATS: pilings, exposed and protected rocky shores, mussel beds

HEIGHT: to 2 in (5 cm)

COLOR: brown, red

One siphon draws in water, while the other expels it. Inside the body cavity a mucus secretion filters the seawater for tiny particles of food. This laden mucus is then passed into the digestive tract, and the nutrients extracted. On some transparent tunicates some of the organs can be seen, including the simple slow-beating heart. When disturbed, the sea squirt retracts, expelling some water, hence its appropriate common name.

Winged Kelp
ALARIA MARGINATA

Winged Kelp is one of the larger brown algae of the West Coast, coming in variable shades of olive-green to dark brown. The long smooth blade has a wavy edge and a strong midrib formed from the stipe, or stalk, at the base. Just above the small but tenacious holdfast is a cluster of smaller blades that are specialized to produce spores. These spores will eventually become whole new kelps. So long is the blade that in rough seas the end is whipped about, giving it a tattered appearance. Winged Kelp is one of the larger and more distinct species of *Alaria* kelps, and it can readily be distinguished from the Sugar Wrack (p. 159) by the dominant midrib running the entire length of the blade.

This kelp makes excellent and nutritious dining, especially for stir-fries and soups or as a wrap for other foods. If biting down on rubbery kelp appeals to you, when harvesting be sure to leave the base of the kelp with its cluster of small reproductive blades. Leaving it alone will allow the kelp to produce many more individuals, and ensure a healthy sustainable harvest.

RANGE: Alaska to Northern California

ZONE: low intertidal, shallow subtidal

HABITATS: rocky shores

LENGTH: to 10 ft (3 m)

WIDTH: to 8 in (20 cm)

COLOR: olive-green, dark brown

Sugar Wrack
LAMINARIA SACCHARINA

This abundant brown kelp thrives in the cool waters of the Northwest, and can be found near the low-tide line and subtidally. A large single blade grows from a stout and strong holdfast that clings to rocks, shells or other algae with its root-like growths. From the holdfast grows a short stipe (sometimes quite long) that broadens into a fine wide blade. Running along the length of mature blades are a series of depressions that give a corrugated effect. This kelp is a rich yellow-brown.

The Sugar Wrack prefers slightly exposed and protected waters where its long blade will not be battered by strong waves. The surface of the kelp many be encrusted with many different organisms, and the holdfast is an excellent hiding place for many creatures that tuck themselves away inside. This kelp gets its name from its sugary taste, and it is used in soups for flavor. In the past it was harvested as an excellent source of iodine, an essential addition to our diet.

RANGE: Alaska to Oregon

ZONE: lower intertidal, shallow subtidal

HABITATS: rocks, sheltered and slightly exposed shores

LENGTH: to 6 ft (1.8 m)

WIDTH: one-quarter of length

COLOR: yellow-brown

Feather Boa
EGREGIA MENZIESII

This exotic brown alga is a common kelp of the exposed and semi-protected coasts from southern British Columbia southwards. One of the largest intertidal brown algae, it grows to impressive lengths. It is noticeable for its many small blades (to 2 inches [5 cm] in length) coming off the side of the main stem, or stipe. Some of these are enlarged into bulbous floats. The illustration shows just one small portion of a long blade. The upper section of the main blade is a golden-brown, while other parts can be olive-green to dark brown.

RANGE: British Columbia to California

ZONE: lower intertidal, shallow subtidal

HABITATS: rocky shores

LENGTH: to 15 ft (4.6 m)

WIDTH: to 6 in (15 cm)

COLOR: olive-green to dark brown

The Shield-backed Kelp Crab (p. 132) often makes its home here, and takes on brown coloration to match the kelp. In addition, a small limpet, less than 1 inch (2.5 cm) in length, lives on the stipe and is found nowhere else. This limpet (*Lottia insessa*) is brown and leaves small depressions in the main stem. It is more common in Oregon and further south, although it does still occur on the Feather Boas of British Columbia. This kelp has often been used as rich mulch, rivaling manure, on farms.

Giant Perennial Kelp
MACROCYSTIS INTEGRIFOLIA

Giant forests of kelp lie just offshore on the open coast where the surf is not too strong. A huge ball of a holdfast ties their great length (to 40 feet [12 m]) down to the seafloor. The stem branches many times, each ending with a series of slim blades. The uppermost section of a kelp frond is illustrated, showing the tapered blades with their bulbous bases. These bulbs are gas-filled, acting as buoyancy to keep the kelp near the surface. The grooved blades, to 2 feet (61 cm) in length, are a deep greenish-brown with toothed edges. New leaf-like blades form by the topmost blade splitting in half repeatedly.

RANGE: Alaska to Southern California

ZONE: low-tide line, subtidal to 33 ft (10 m)

HABITATS: rocky shores

LENGTH: to 40 ft (12 m)

COLOR: dark greenish-brown

The kelp forest's immense productivity is harvested off some coasts—but only the top 3 feet (91 cm) are taken, allowing the kelp to continue growing. This kelp produces 'algin,' a substance with many uses such as giving ice cream the right texture. Storms also take their usual cut of weaker kelp, casting them up in huge piles of wrack. Refer to the Sea Otter (p. 31) for a story about the past demise of these great forests.

Bull Kelp

NEREOCYSTIS LUETKEANA

A common brown alga of the West Coast, the Bull Kelp is also one of the most popular. It has some impressive statistics, growing up to 80 feet (24 m) long, and is secured by a massive holdfast that is as much as 16 inches (41 cm) across. Most incredible is that all this growth occurs in one summer season. By early winter the kelp are dying, and storms toss their distinctive form up on shores where beachcombers are enthralled by them.

A very obvious feature is the large bulbous float that is up to 4.5 inches (11 cm) in diameter. This thick-walled vessel is filled with gas and keeps the lengthy fronds afloat. At low tide, they can be seen bobbing in the gentle waves just offshore. The tough hollow stipes take months to rot, and have been used as fishing line in the past. The dark greenish-brown blades grow off two nodes on the float, and reach a length of 10 feet (3 m). Stranded stipes, when sliced and pickled, are excellent to eat.

OTHER NAME: Bull Whip

RANGE: Alaska to Southern California

ZONE: shallow subtidal

HABITATS: rocky exposed shores

LENGTH: to 80 ft (24 m)

COLOR: dark greenish-brown

Sea Palm

POSTELSIA PALMAEFORMIS

O n the most exposed rocks where the surf smashes in full force, the Sea Palm can be seen growing in tree-like groves. A thick rubbery stem bends with the force of the waves, springing back up once each wave subsides. From the top of the hollow stem numerous flattened blades hang down. Young Sea Palms are green, but as they age they take on the brownish hues typical of the brown algae family. These are annual plants, living only one summer season and growing from fresh seeds every year.

Their exposed location requires a tough holdfast that sends root-like extensions into the rocky crevices. California Mussel (p. 90) and Acorn Barnacle (p. 135) beds are frequently interspersed with clusters of this beautiful kelp. The Sea Palm makes an excellent addition to stir-fries, and is just as good eaten fresh. But its location is a hazardous one, so be sure to keep an eye on the surf if you are tempted to grab a handful. In addition, don't take too much—you will jeopardize the ability of that grove to regenerate next year.

RANGE: British Columbia to California

ZONE: upper to middle intertidal

HABITATS: exposed rocky shores

HEIGHT: to 20 in (51 cm)

COLOR: green to olive-brown

Black Pine
RHODOMELA LARIX

Almost black when dry, this alga is rich brown when wet. It thrives on protected rocky shores from the middle to lower intertidal zone throughout the region, and is found on rocks or in tidepools. It gets its name from the short needle-like clusters of branches coming off the main stem, or stipe. These clusters are spirally arranged around the cylindrical stipe. The growth habit of these needles resembles the larch tree, whose genus name, *Larix*, is the inspiration for the scientific name for this brown alga.

In winter the 'needles' drop off, leaving bare stems. They grow back next spring. Several stipes will grow from one small holdfast. Sometimes attached to the dense growth is the brown alga *Soranthera ulvoidea*. This alga is easily recognizable when it is mature, since it forms a large bulbous growth almost 2 inches (5 cm) across. The dense growth of the Black Pine also makes an ideal hiding place for many small crustaceans. Be sure to compare this alga with the Fir Needle, which has flatter 'needles.'

RANGE: Alaska to Northern California

ZONE: middle to lower intertidal

HABITATS: rocky shores, sheltered shores

LENGTH: to 12 in (30 cm)

COLOR: dark brown, blackish

SIMILAR SPECIES: Fir Needle (p. 167)

Little Rockweed
PELVETIOPSIS LIMITATA

The Little Rockweed can be mistaken for its larger cousin *Fucus distichus*, but a few features distinguish it. This seaweed grows in small clumps, often with upright stems, while larger *Fucus* hangs down. The stipe may branch once or a few times before ending in two swollen receptacles (reproductive organs) filled with spores, while *Fucus* has much longer stems with more branching and more bulbous receptacles. Little Rockweed lacks a midrib and only grows to a height or length of 6 inches (15 cm), seldom having the weight or length to droop over.

This brown alga stands out on the shore because it is often a bright olive-green or yellowish-brown, and is found in the high intertidal zone on rocky shores. Its preference is for the exposed and wave-swept rocky coasts from British Columbia to California, and it will not be found where the surf is seldom rough. Like *Fucus*, it has a mucus coating to protect it from desiccation. These stout shoots are an excellent and tasty addition to stir-fries and soups.

RANGE: British Columbia to Northern California

ZONE: upper intertidal

HABITATS: rocky exposed shores

LENGTH: to 6 in (15 cm)

COLOR: olive-green, yellowish-brown

SIMILAR SPECIES: Rockweed (*Fucus distichus*) (p. 166)

Rockweed
FUCUS DISTICHUS

Anyone clambering about the rocks when the tide is out will have come across the successful Rockweeds. There are several species all quite similar in form, and they typically grow on rocks in the middle intertidal zone. Thick drooping clumps hang down from the tops of rocks in shades of olive-green to yellowish-green, and almost black when they dry out. This alga is a member of the brown algae family, despite having greenish tones! A shoot grows from a tiny holdfast and then repeatedly divides. At the end of each branch is a swollen 'receptacle' where sex cells are produced. These are inflated, and when slightly dry, pop and explode under foot—a popular pastime for some younger beachcombers.

OTHER NAMES: Bladderwrack; Popping Wrack

RANGE: Alaska to Southern California

ZONE: middle intertidal

HABITATS: rocky shores

LENGTH: to 20 in (51 cm)

COLOR: olive-green, yellowish-green

SIMILAR SPECIES: Little Rockweed (p. 165)

Walking over rocks covered in this seaweed is hazardous—it produces slimy mucus to keep it from drying out. This makes the rocks devilishly slippery. Be sure to lift up the dangling fronds—underneath it is very moist and all kinds of organisms will be taking refuge here while the tide is out. A common twisting version of Rockweed is *Fucus spiralis*.

Fir Needle
ANALIPAS JAPONICUS

We tend to think of algae as being green so they can harness the sun's light. Marine algae can be green, but also brown and red. This is a brown alga, with dark pigments masking the green pigments that are still present. Pigments are variable, and the Fir Needle can range from reddish-brown to pale olive-green. Several stems form from one encrusting holdfast, giving it a bushy appearance. From each stem arise many flattened 'branches' that resemble fir needles. These bushy clumps drape over rocks on moderately exposed shores at low tide.

The Japanese have long used this seaweed, which goes by the name 'matsuma,' for food. When harvested it is packed in salt to preserve it, and then cooked in soy sauce. The salted seaweed is also layered with edible mushrooms to preserve them. This seaweed is an excellent source for protein and minerals, but can only be harvested between May and November. As winter encroaches, the shoots die off, but the little holdfast remains, throwing up new growth the following spring.

RANGE: Alaska to Northern California

ZONE: middle to lower intertidal

HABITATS: moderately exposed rocky shores

STEM LENGTH: to 10 in (25 cm)

BRANCH LENGTH: to 1 in (2.5 cm)

COLOR: olive-green to dark brown

SIMILAR SPECIES: Black Pine (p. 164)

Tar Spot
RALFSIA PACIFICA

I t's hard to believe that these encrusting dark brown or black spots are another species of brown alga—they are so easy to step over and ignore. They form thin encrusting growths on rocks of the middle to lower intertidal zone. Most take on a circular shape, gradually growing outwards. Close inspection of the surface may reveal tiny lines radiating from the central point, as well as concentric ridges. Even under a microscope it is hard to believe that this is really an alga. It is composed of thin layers of cells and tiny threads, all packed in with a tough coat.

RANGE: Alaska to Southern California
ZONE: middle to lower intertidal
HABITATS: rocky shores
DIAMETER: to 8 in (20 cm)
COLOR: dark brown, black
SIMILAR SPECIES: Blobs of Tar (p. 180)

These algae are highly tolerant of extreme conditions. Their dark colors ensure that they absorb most of the sun's radiation, and they become very hot. A tough outer coating helps protect them. Other species of similar encrusting algae may be encountered in shades of red and brown. This one might easily be mistaken for the aftermath of an oil spill, but rest assured, this time it is an alga!

Sea Staghorn
CODIUM FRAGILE

This distinctive green alga is often seen perched on the top or sides of rocks. It is a very dark green, almost black, and the velvety texture feels more like a sponge. From a small holdfast, columnar branches grow, and these branches repeatedly divide in two, giving that antler-like quality. The branches are firm and rounded, standing upright when young. As they grow longer, they droop with their own weight. A dusting of white occurs on some branches.

On close inspection you might notice the sea slug *Elysia hedgpethi* that lives on this alga. The green pigment (chlorophyll) that it swallows while eating the alga continues to photosynthesize for some time, perhaps offering sugary nutrition to the slug. The alga is highly nutritious, loaded with vitamins and iron. In Japan it is sugared and eaten as a delicacy, or used in soups and as a garnish. Loved in Japan, it is hated by the fisheries of the East Coast—shellfish bind to it readily, then the alga breaks off in storms and the valuable crop is lost to the sea.

RANGE: Alaska to Southern California

ZONE: middle to lower intertidal, shallow subtidal

HABITATS: rocky shores

LENGTH: to 16 in (41 cm)

COLOR: very dark green

Enteromorpha Green Algae

ENTEROMORPHA SPP.

Pools along the highest splash-line of the waves are not easy places to live in. Filled with rainwater one minute and engulfed in sea spray the next, they suffer the beating sun and freezing snowfalls, too. One group of algae thrives under these trying conditions, and does well enough that whole pools can be filled with the dazzling green tangles of Enteromorpha. Tubular strands of algae can be seen along seepages in the cliffs, on mudflats and estuaries—most often where fresh water and seawater mix.

The fragile strands often fill with bubbles of oxygen, making them float on the surface of the pools. Several forms of these algae occur, all bright green or yellow-green and with either long thin tubes or flattened wider strands. When they die they lose the green chlorophyll pigments and turn a ghostly white. Found worldwide, many cultures eat these algae because they are highly nutritious. If you are tempted, be very cautious— these highly tolerant algae frequently grow in polluted water.

OTHER NAME: Confetti

RANGE: Alaska to Northern California

ZONE: above high-tide line

HABITATS: spraypools, brackish water, seepages, estuaries, mud-flats

LENGTH: to 10 in (25 cm)

COLOR: brilliant green, yellow-green

SIMILAR SPECIES: Sea Lettuce (p.171)

Sea Lettuce

ULVA SPP.

Bright green and frilled, this alga has earned the name Sea Lettuce. It is edible and eaten as a rich source of vitamins and minerals in some parts of the world. The blades of the alga are only two cells thick, and are consequently translucent. When the oblong sheets dry out, they crinkle. Sea Lettuce attaches to rocks from the upper to lower intertidal zone, but is confined to tidepools in the upper zone. It can be seen gently drifting on mudflats and in estuaries, bays and lagoons.

There are several species of *Ulva*, or maybe not—biologists have yet to decide just how many we are dealing with. Some come as uniform sheets, while others are perforated with holes and have tatty edges. It turns up on other seaweeds, and occasionally attaches to the Pacific Plate Limpet (p. 50). If the water has gone green in a tidepool, the Sea Lettuce has released its tiny reproductive cells from the edges of the blades. Equally as green, Enteromorpha Green Algae grow as fine strands.

RANGE: Alaska to Southern California

ZONE: upper to lower intertidal

HABITATS: rocky shores, tidepools, calm waters

LENGTH: to 20 in (51 cm)

COLOR: bright green

SIMILAR SPECIES: Enteromorpha Green Algae (p. 170)

Nail Brush

ENDOCLADIA MURICATA

This very common alga has predominantly red pigments and appears dark red to purple, sometimes brown. It favors the very high reaches of the shore where it clings to the rocks in the close company of the hardy Acorn Barnacles (p. 135). Here, it is exposed to the rigors of intertidal life, drying up in hot sunshine. As it dries out, the colors become very dark, almost black, and the thin branches shrivel. When wet it is soft and supple, but when dry it is coarse and wiry. These are hardy tufts of algae, some of which may not feel the spray of the ocean for more than a day, because they grow so high in the intertidal zone.

OTHER NAME: Sea Moss

RANGE: Alaska to Southern California

ZONE: upper intertidal

HABITATS: rocky shores

HEIGHT: to 3 in (7.6 cm)

COLOR: dark red, purple, black

Little clumps, resembling woodland moss, scatter the rocks of exposed and partially protected shores. The fine texture is made from many slender branches, each of which is covered by tiny spines. These dense little forests are well worth poking into, because many tiny creatures crawl inside the tangle to take shelter from predators and the elements.

Turkish Towel
GIGARTINA EXASPERATA

Turkish Towels are an attractive addition to rocky and cobble shores, where their splashes of red add to the browns and greens in the mats of seaweed. When very young the color is intense and bright, but as it ages, the seaweed becomes a very dark purple-red, losing its brilliance, and sometimes appearing almost black. The blades are long and wide, and covered in small nodules that give it a rough texture like a coarse towel. When submerged or very wet, the blades have an iridescent bluish sheen.

Several species of *Gigartina* grow on our shores from Alaska to California. They are only obvious in summer when the blades rapidly expand from small growths on the holdfast. In winter the blades die off and are a frequent addition to the wrack on the beaches after a storm. The little holdfast sits tight through winter, waiting for spring and new growth. Turkish Towels are an excellent source of carrageenan, an agent that is used in industry and foods for so many different applications.

RANGE: British Columbia to Southern California

ZONE: lower intertidal, subtidal to 60 ft (18 m)

HABITATS: rocky shores, cobbles

LENGTH: to 18 in (46 cm)

WIDTH: to 10 in (25 cm)

COLOR: bright red to very dark purple-red

Sea Sac

HALOSACCION GLANDIFORME

The peculiar Sea Sac can be seen in distinctive clumps on rocky shores. Because of the pigments it uses to harness the sun's light, it belongs in the family of red algae. Just to confuse you it more often appears olive-green, but sometimes brownish, and if you look near the base, you might see some reddish tints. The clumps resemble bunches of fingers or sausages, and they often grow in a distinct band along rocky shores of exposed and sheltered coasts. This band occurs in the middle intertidal zone. Such a distinct band is a good example of intertidal zonation, with each plant or animal specifically tied to one part of the zone owing to competition, predation or physical factors.

RANGE: Alaska to Southern California
ZONE: middle intertidal
HABITATS: rocky shores
LENGTH: to 6 in (15 cm)
COLOR: olive-green, brown, reddish

The bulbous sacs arise from a tiny holdfast and are usually filled with water. At the top of sac there is often a bubble. This is an accumulation of gases made during photosynthesis on bright days. If you give the sac a gentle squeeze, watch out for the tiny jets of water forced out of small pores in the thin wall of the plant.

Iridescent Seaweed
IRIDAEA CORDATA

This beautiful seaweed comes deep red overlaid with an iridescence that gives tints of purple, blue and green to the fleshy blade. From a small holdfast comes one dominant blade with several smaller blades that are all slippery-smooth. The edges undulate and are often torn by the action of the waves. Very young blades are blue. In winter, they die back, just leaving the sturdy holdfast from which new blades will grow the following spring.

A newcomer to this alga would be forgiven for thinking that the oily sheen was from the aftermath of an oil spill—this beautiful phenomenon is entirely the product of nature.

RANGE: Alaska to Southern California

ZONE: lower intertidal, shallow subtidal

HABITATS: rocky shores

LENGTH: to 36 in (91 cm)

COLOR: deep red, iridescent

Like the Turkish Towel (p. 173), this seaweed is loaded with carrageenan. Research is under way to establish profitable and practical ways to commercially grow this alga. Such research is important, because it may offer a way of growing the seaweed without us having to rape and pillage the shores for it, and consequently damage the habitats for many other organisms.

Coralline Algae

CORALLINA SPP.

Carpets of Coralline Algae coat the bottom and sides of some tidepools. Where other seaweeds get chewed to bits, these tough ones are left alone. The tidepool residents just don't enjoy them. Often feathery in appearance, these algae have a very tough texture resulting from heavily calcified walls. Cells deposit so much lime (calcium carbonate) that early naturalists thought they were studying a type of coral animal and not a plant!

RANGE: Alaska to Southern California

ZONE: lower intertidal, shallow subtidal

HABITATS: rocky shores, open coasts

LENGTH: to 4 in (10 cm)

COLOR: bright pink to dark purple

Bright pink to deep purple, the fronds are often edged in white. These jointed branches arise from a flat encrusting growth spreading over the rock. Most of the alga is rigid, but at the joints there is less lime, and some flexibility is an advantage when the rough surf crashes in. There are many different species of Coralline Algae never growing to more than a few inches in length. When they die, they rapidly bleach white. Most Coralline Algae avoid being eaten because of their toughness, but some Coralline Algae grow as encrustations that may be grazed by some snails.

Encrusting Coral

LITHOTHAMNIUM PACIFICUM

Often overlooked, these pretty crusts are not strange rocks, but algae related to the Coralline Algae (p. 176). Forming small patches of tough growths, they might merge to create large colonies, overlapping and growing on top of one another. Usually pink, this alga also comes in deep purple, and the edges or nodules on its surface may be fringed in white.

An encrusting resident of rocks, it will also grow on shells and is commonly seen near the low-tide line, especially in tidepools.

Many patches have knobs on the surface and small white dots may be evident. It is from these dots that microscopic spores emerge to start new encrustations. The crustiness of this alga is attributed to heavy deposits of lime (calcium carbonate) that it extracts from seawater. Despite being so hard, it does fall prey to some mollusks. The White-cap Limpet (p. 45) lives on it, and is frequently overgrown with it, and the extravagantly marked Lined Chiton (p. 95) adheres to it, grazing slowly and adopting pinkish coloration to blend in with the alga.

OTHER NAME: Pink Rock Crusts

RANGE: British Columbia to Southern California

ZONE: low-tide line, shallow subtidal

HABITATS: rocks, shells, tidepools

DIAMETER: variable to several inches (cm)

COLOR: white, pink, purple

Surf Grass
PHYLLOSPADIX SPP.

O n rocky shores huge beds of Surf Grass sway back and forth with the wash of waves. These vivid green leaves are not those of algae, but rather of flowering plants just like some relatives on land. They have a root system instead of a holdfast, and require sediments to sink their roots into. The leaves are long, slim and a brilliant green, and the flowers are nestled tightly against the stems. There are two common species of Surf Grass that are essentially similar.

RANGE: Alaska to Southern California

ZONE: middle to lower intertidal, shallow subtidal

HABITATS: rocky shores, open coasts

LENGTH: to 36 in (91 cm)

COLOR: green

SIMILAR SPECIES: Eelgrass (p. 179)

Surf Grass beds are excellent habitats to poke around in. A small isopod (*Idotea montereyensis*), resembling Vosnesensky's Isopod (p. 141), clings to the leaves and matches the green color. Shield-backed Kelp Crabs (p. 132) can be seen tenaciously grasping with their long legs as the leaves sway back and forth. Thick beds of Surf Grass are a favored hiding place for some crabs at low tide. Sometimes the vivid green color is masked by an excessive growth of a fuzzy red alga, *Smithora naiadum*. Surf Grass resembles Eelgrass, but needs rocky wave-swept coasts and not the calmer sandy waters of Eelgrass.

Eelgrass
ZOSTERA MARINA

D on some waders and be sure to gently walk through the extensive Eelgrass meadows of quiet bays. Eelgrass prefers water with a gentle flow where some fresh water has mixed with the sea. Like Surf Grass, which it resembles, Eelgrass is a flowering plant. The green leaves are strap-like, with inconspicuous flowers tucked near the stems. Eelgrass spreads through muddy sand with rhizomes from which new plants grow.

The thick mat stabilizes the soft mud, and is easy to walk on. The meadows are rewarding for the diverse wildlife they harbor. These are perfect nurseries for young fish, and crabs such as the Dungeness (p. 128) and Shield-backed Kelp crabs (p. 132). Anemones wave their tentacles, while snails graze upon all kinds of encrustations and smother the leaves and stems. Nudibranchs creep about and pulsing jellyfish drift by. Shrimp dart around your feet. Clams have siphons peaking above the muddy surface and sea stars, including the massive Sunflower Star (p. 112), cruise along the bottom in search of prey. A meadow of Eelgrass is wildlife at your feet, and you don't have to watch out for dangerous waves!

RANGE: Alaska to Southern California

ZONE: low intertidal, shallow subtidal

HABITATS: quiet bays, muddy bottom

LENGTH: to 36 in (91 cm)

COLOR: green

SIMILAR SPECIES: Surf Grass (p. 178)

Blobs of Tar
HOMINIS POLLUTANTISSIMUM

Beachcombing does come with minor hazards. Watch out for Blobs of Tar! These globular black masses hide in sand, or stick to rocks. Try to avoid them if you can, because they are sticky and hard to remove. Get some on your skin and you will be scrubbing like crazy. Get some on your clothes and you may as well throw them away. They can be tenacious and long lasting. Don't confuse them with the all-natural algal Tar Spots.

RANGE: Alaska to Southern California

ZONE: upper to lower intertidal, offshore

HABITATS: anywhere, floating

LENGTH: microscopic to miles (km) across

COLOR: usually oily black

SIMILAR SPECIES: Tar Spot (p. 168)

Unfortunately, our beautiful oceans suffer from human activities in many ways. Blobs of Tar are tiny versions of larger problems—oil slicks.

Tankers have accidents and oil, in its various forms, pours onto the oceans, sticking to the feathers of birds and the soft fur of otters. These animals get waterlogged and die. Fish and shellfish suffocate, and many creatures are slowly poisoned. Oil is just one example of our neglect of the oceans. Remember that our oceans are sacred and think about your actions when you visit. Respect all wildlife and water, and please take all that garbage home with you.

Glossary

anal fin
the fin running underneath the fish behind the anus, but in front of the tail

aperture
the opening to the shell of gastropods out of which the animal emerges

bivalve
group of mollusks possessing two valves or shells that enclose the animal

byssal threads
tough threads made of strong protein secreted by some bivalves to attach themselves firmly to rocks

calcareous
whitish deposits or material made from calcium carbonate (lime), like shells

calcium carbonate
white, hard compound extracted from the sea to make shells, also called lime.

carapace
large, flat portion of the crab's shell covering the head and thorax from which the legs arise; often washed ashore after molting

carnivore
consumes other animals or parts of them

cerata
fleshy growths on the back of some nudibranchs, usually with an extension of the gut running inside

cirrus
hand-like appendages, or small, hairy growths; used in reference to growths on fish heads and the feathery feet of barnacles for filter feeding

commensal
where one organism lives with, in or on another, gaining some advantages such as food or shelter, without harming its host

GLOSSARY

crustacean
group of arthropods, including the crabs, shrimp and beach fleas

encrustation
usually a low, flat, firm growth (crust) covering a surface

estuarine
where a fresh water river exits into the sea; salinity drops because the salts are diluted by the fresh water, and both sea and river influence local geography

filter feeder
an organism that feeds using feathered or net-like appendages, or other means, to extract tiny or even microscopic particles suspended in the water

gastropod
molluskan snails, such as whelks, dogwinkles and limpets

girdle
fleshy band surrounding the plates of chitons

herbivore
consumes plants or parts of plants

holdfast
root-like structure with which seaweeds attach themselves to rocky substrates

intertidal zone
zone between low-tide line and high-tide line

mantle
sheet of living tissue that secretes the shells of snails and encloses the delicate gills

midrib
central rib running the length of some blades of kelp (absent in other species)

nematocyst
specialized stinging cells found in the tentacles of jellyfish, anemones and corals

nocturnal
active by night

nudibranch
another name for sea slug

omnivore
consumes pretty much anything it wants to, provided it is worth it

operculum
a horny door with which a gastropod shuts itself in; used to protect against predators, and to prevent from drying out during low tide

periostracum
tough organic layer on the shell of mollusks

plankton
tiny organisms suspended in water drifting at the mercy of the currents and tides

radula
tooth-like structure used for scraping or boring, taking on various forms depending on the diet of the gastropod or chiton

red tide
occasional blooms of a single-celled organism causes reddening of water; toxins from these organisms build up in the flesh of shellfish; not a toxin you want to consume

rhinophores
sensory structures, like tentacles, on the head of nudibranchs

salinity
level of salt in water; high salinity means lots of sea salt

sessile
sitting, or fixed, usually incapable of moving around, as in the case of barnacles and mussels

silica
hard mineral, like quartz and glass, occurring in sponge spicules

siphons
tube-like extensions from mollusks to obtain water that is drawn into the mantle cavity; particularly evident in burrowing bivalves

stipe
seaweed equivalent of a stem

test
tough supporting structure, or skeleton, of echinoderms, such as the Eccentric Sand Dollars found on beaches

umbo
located near the hinge of bivalve mollusks is the oldest part of the mollusk, often prominent and beak-like

valve
one half, or shell, of a bivalve

whorl
one complete turn of a spire on a snail shell

zooplankton
animal component of plankton (the plant element being phytoplankton)

zooid
individual member of a bryozoan colony

Further Reading

Behrens, David W. 1980. *Pacific Coast Nudibranchs*. Los Osos, California: Sea Challengers.

Delphine, Haley (ed). 1978. *Marine Mammals of the Eastern North Pacific and Arctic Waters*. Seattle, Washington: Pacific Search Press.

Eschmeyer, William, N. and Earl S. Herald. 1983. *Pacific Coast Fishes*. Peterson Field Guide Series. Boston, Massachusetts: Houghton Mifflin Company.

Goodson, Car. 1988. *Fishes of the Pacific Coast*. Stanford, California: Stanford University Press.

Gotshall, Daniel, W. 1994. *Guide to Marine Invertebrates: Alaska to Baja California*. Monterey, California: Sea Challengers.

Harbo, Rick M. 1997. *Shells and Shellfish of the Pacific Northwest*. Madeira Park, British Columbia: Harbour Publishing.

Jensen, Gregory C. 1995. *Pacific Coast Crabs and Shrimps*. Monterey, California: Sea Challengers.

Kozloff, Eugene, N. 1993. *Seashore Life of the Northern Pacific Coast: an illustrated guide to Northern California, Oregon, Washington and British Columbia*. Seattle, Washington: University of Washington Press.

Lamb, Andrew. 1986. *Coastal Fishes of the Pacific Northwest*. Madeira Park, British Columbia: Harbour Publishing.

Love, Milton. 1996. *Probably More Than You Want to Know About the Fishes of the Pacific Coast*. Santa Barbara, California: Really Big Press.

McConnaughey, B.H. and E. McConnaughey. 1988. *Pacific Coast*. The Audubon Society Nature Guides. New York: Alfred A. Knopf.

Morris, Percy, A. 1980. *Pacific Coast Shells*. Peterson Field Guide Series. Boston, Massachusetts: Houghton Mifflin Company.

Niesen, Thomas, M. 1997. *Beachcomber's Guide to Marine Life of the Pacific Northwest*. Houston, Texas: Gulf Publishing Company.

Paine, Stephanie Hewlett. 1992. *Beachwalker: Sea Life of the West Coast*. Vancouver/Toronto: Douglas & McIntyre.

Ricketts, Edward F. and Jack Calvin. 1968. *Between Pacific Tides*. Stanford, California: Stanford University Press.

Waaland, J. Robert. 1977. *Common Seaweeds of the Pacific Coast*. Seattle, Washington: Pacific Search Press.

Index

Page numbers in bold typeface indicate primary, illustrated species.

INDEX

INDEX

INDEX

About the Author

Ian Sheldon has lived in South Africa, Singapore, Britain and Canada. Caught collecting caterpillars at the age of three, he has been exposed to the beauty and diversity of nature ever since. He was educated at Cambridge University, England, and the University of Alberta, Canada. When he is not in the tropics working on conservation projects or immersing himself in our beautiful wilderness, he is sharing his love for nature. An accomplished artist, naturalist and educator, Ian enjoys communicating passion through the visual arts and the written word, in the hope that he will inspire love and affection for all nature.

MORE GREAT BOOKS
ABOUT THE OUTDOORS!